Table of Contents

From Party Animal to Rational Animal

From the time I was a junior in high school until I was a freshman in college, I had many long and deep conversations with a close friend from Brazil, Felipe. Felipe asked me questions that caused me to have a lot of doubts about my Catholic faith. I never got to a point where I actually would have claimed "God does not exist," but looking back I would say that I was basically agnostic. I didn't know what I really believed or what I could really know for sure, and I was heavily influenced by Felipe's relativistic attitude towards truth and knowledge. A few years ago, I had become depressed and dissatisfied with the lack of meaning in my life, because I was working a job that I thought was pointless, going to school to get a job that I couldn't see myself actually doing everyday, spending most of my nights drinking and partying, and many of my mornings with a regretful conscience and a throbbing brain.

Facing the Facts

Finally, I started to ask myself the tough questions like, "Is this all there is in life? Hating Mondays and loving Fridays? Mechanically going through the motions of life, punching your time card, checking the boxes, motivated only by the next opportunity to get a 12-pack and play video games?" Somehow I had the honesty to admit that, if God does not exist, then the answer to these questions is, ultimately, "Yes, this is it." This was a frightening realization to me, like the harsh reality we face at a funeral. We know in the back of our minds that we will all die someday, but that fact is brought into the light when we get that diagnosis, that phone call, or we have to carry that casket. The Catholic apologist Matt Fradd said in his story of conversion from agnosticism, "When you die, people will talk about you the same way you talk about people who are dead now." Like the motivation that comes from the realization of one's own mortality, the thought that my life might be meaningless motivated me. It motivated me to search for the truth about God, reality, and the purpose of my life.

Enter Philosophy

On my search for meaning and purpose I quickly came across the work of Dr. William Lane Craig. Dr. Craig is a Christian (evangelical protestant) philosopher of religion and time. He has written many books, and has also participated in many debates with some of the most prominent atheists of today, including the late Christopher Hitchens (who died in 2011), theoretical physicist Lawrence Krauss, and neuroscientist Sam Harris. The argument that Dr. Craig is probably most famous for defending is the Kalāam Cosmological Argument (hereafter KCA). The KCA is a deductive argument for the existence of God. The argument was originally formulated and defended by Muslims during the Middle Ages, and the word "kalaam" means "speech" in Arabic. The argument is simple, containing just three steps:

1. Whatever begins to exist has a cause for its existence.
2. The universe began to exist.
3. Therefore, the universe has a cause for its existence.

Until modern times, the truth of the major (first) premise was more or less taken for granted. The idea that "nothing comes from nothing" seems so self-evident that most people find it almost redundant to even mention. This is, however, the goal of the first premise in an argument, to begin with something that your opponent will almost certainly agree with. The second premise was the one that received most of the criticism. Realize that, until the Big Bang Theory was proposed by Belgian priest Fr. Georges Lemaître, and observational evidence found to support it in the late 1920s, virtually all scientists believed that the universe was eternal, that is to say, that the universe had existed for an infinite amount of time into the past. Dr. Craig points out that the idea of an actually infinite past is very strange and has many paradoxical implications. For example, imagine you are waiting for a particular domino (which represents today) to fall in a row of dominoes. But, imagine that there are literally an infinite amount of dominoes that must fall before that domino can fall. How would that domino ever fall if you had to wait for an infinite amount of dominoes to fall before it? In other words, if the past is infinite, how did we manage to get through an infinite number of days in order to get to the present day? The impossibility of such a scenario, known as an "infinite regress," provides good reason to think that the universe must have had a beginning, without even getting into the empirical evidence that has been discovered in more recent times.

The Worst Birthday Present Ever

In 2007, at the famous theoretical physicist Stephen Hawking's 70th birthday party, prominent cosmologist Alexander Vilenkin presented a theorem titled the "Borde, Vilenkin, and Guthe (BVG) Theorem." The BVG theorem, developed by Vilenkin and his colleagues, proved with a very high level of scientific certainty that any universe that was expanding would have to have a beginning in time. Vilenkin pulled no punches when he put forth the proof, saying this after he had presented it:

> It is said that an argument will convince a reasonable man, and that a proof will convince even an unreasonable man. Now that the proof is in place [referring to the BVG theorem], physicists and cosmologists can no longer hide behind even the possibility that the universe is past infinite. There is no escape. They must face the reality of a beginning . . . To view an inflationary universe without a beginning is impossible.

Once he had heard the proof explained, the birthday boy Stephen Hawking exclaimed, "My goodness! It has very transcendent implications!" No kidding! One journalist writing about the event in New Scientist magazine titled her article "Why Physicists Can't Avoid a Creation Event: The Worst Birthday Present Ever." With more and more evidence mounting to support the idea that the universe did in fact begin to exist, some physicists and cosmologists, worried about these implications, have resorted to attacking the first premise, that "Whatever begins to exist has a cause for its existence." The fact that they would go so far as to reject one of the most basic principals in philosophy, the "principal of sufficient reason," which maintains that every effect must have a cause that explains it, reveals how strong their prior commitment is to an uncreated universe.

Let Nothing Be Nothing

If the universe really did begin to exist, then that would mean that prior to its absolute beginning, the universe was literally *nothing*. While it may sound simple enough, it is important to understand what is meant by the word "nothing." Nothing is the complete absence of being, and it has no properties or potentialities, that is, it does not have in itself the potential to become something. It is not the low-energy state of a quantum field or a vacuum, both of which have properties, namely, that they are conditioned by time. It is also not a void, because you can have more or less of a void, and a void is dimensional and orientable. One scientist once joked, "nothing is the stuff rocks dream about." So, if the universe was really nothing before it began to exist, then it could not have moved itself from nothing to something—that would imply that it could do something. There would have to be a transcendent cause, a cause outside of the universe, that brought the universe into existence out of nothing. Also, since there is literally an infinite gap between nothing and something, we can infer that the transcendent cause would have to be all-powerful or omnipotent (sound familiar?). Suppose someone is still willing to deny the first premise and say that something can come from nothing. This raises the question, "What is it about nothing that makes it only able to produce universes?" In other words, if something can come from nothing, then why have we never observed it? Why don't random planets, objects, molecules, or even BMW's and Border Collies pop into being out of nothing? This might sound silly, but that is only because it is perfectly consistent with a silly notion, the notion that something could come from nothing.

Fides et Ratio (Faith and Reason)

In conclusion, I believe the KCA is sound and that it has strong theistic (or at least deistic) implications for anyone who is willing to study it honestly (key word: honestly). It is important to realize that the KCA, along with other arguments for the existence of God, does not in any way prove the existence of the Judeo-Christian God, or any particular god, but it does prove the existence of an all-powerful and transcendent cause of the universe, which is enough to refute the atheist or to reassure the person doubting God's existence. In dialogue with atheists or agnostics, it is important to remember that, once you sort through all of the rhetorical and often times emotionally charged arguments, every argument against the existence of God will be claiming one of two things: 1) that the past can be infinite, or 2) that something can come from nothing – both of which are problematic propositions and extremely difficult to support by reasoned argumentation. Thanks be to God, for all of Creation, and for giving us the ability to reason our way to knowing that He exists, as the Church maintains in her Catechism: "The existence of God the Creator can be known with certainty through his works, by the light of human reason" (*CCC* 286). Saint Paul wrote the following about unbelievers in his letter to the Romans:

> For what can be known about God is plain to them, because God has shown it to them. Ever since the creation of the world his invisible nature, namely, his eternal power and deity, has been clearly perceived in the things that have been made (Rm 1:19-20).

† Under the Mercy,

Chris Trummer

Sources:

Catholic Church. *Catechism of the Catholic Church*. 2nd Ed. Washington, DC: United States Catholic Conference, 2000. Print.

Grossman, Lisa. "Why physicists can't avoid a creation event." New Scientist. Retrieved on 11-11-2014. URL: http://www.newscientist.com/article/mg21328474.400-why-physicists-cant-avoid-a-creation-event.html. Web.

What's Your Foundation?

When trying to convince someone about the morality (or immorality) of a given action, there often seems to be little progress made. In my experience, this is usually the result of the other person having different beliefs about the foundation of moral values and duties. As a Catholic Christian, I believe that moral values and duties are objective realities created by God. They are not arbitrary "rules" that God made up – they flow from God's very nature. If God is the *Summum Bonum* or Highest Good, and He created the universe for a purpose, it follows that an action carried out in His Creation is objectively good and moral to the extent that it conforms to His purpose. It is very inconsistent (and sometimes, comical) when skeptics or atheists try to maintain the existence of objective moral values and duties, that is, "values and duties that are real and binding on all people, regardless of time, place, or culture," without God as their source.

Missing the Point

This is the most misunderstood aspect of Christian morality. Non-believers will often say, "I don't need to believe in God to be a good person," "Why can't we just be good people and leave religion out of this?" and, "Isn't it better to just be good because you want to, instead of doing so because some two-thousand-year-old book tells you to, or because you're afraid of going to Hell?" The truth is, no reasonable Christian will claim that an atheist or agnostic cannot live their life in a moral way, and the only thing statements and questions like these prove is that the person offering them is completely missing the point of the argument. The argument is NOT that belief in God is necessary for a person to act morally. Rather, it is that the existence of God is necessary.

In a world plagued by moral relativism, the one authority that everyone still believes they must obey is their own conscience. By conscience I mean the faculty every human being has by nature to judge the moral quality of actions and distinguish right from wrong. Personally, I find this universal obedience to conscience somewhat curious. Why does conscience have this authority? To answer this, we must look at the possible sources of conscience. They are:

1. Nature, as in beliefs about behavior learned through the evolutionary process
2. Ourselves, as in our personal tastes and subjective interpretations
3. Society, as in social norms formed by the majority opinion
4. An external, higher source like a transcendent Creator

"Follow Your ~~Conscience~~ Biological Processes"

If the source of our moral conscience is evolution, that would mean that all of the moral values and duties that we encounter in life are merely the products of random mutation and natural selection, and that what we perceive as our "conscience" is really just highly developed natural instincts that best served our ancestors in allowing them to survive and reproduce. If this really were the case, then how can I be bound to follow my conscience? Why should I be obligated to answer to a biological process? Why should I believe that the instincts I've inherited from thousands upon thousands of years ago are a trustworthy guide to follow, or authority to obey, when deciding how I will conduct myself? The fact is, the processes of nature, as beautiful and intricate as they are, cannot be binding on my conscience. Also, what is widely regarded as morally reprehensible is often times what our instinct tells us to do, and yet we resist through good judgement and experience. Our conscience is less like a factory installed computer program, which operates in a fixed and predetermined way, and more like a seed that is planted in us, which we must nourish and help grow, or else neglect and let decay.

It's Not MY Truth, It's THE Truth

What if we just make up morality for ourselves? You can have your "truth," and I'll have mine. That way we can all be considered moral and avoid having to deal with others who try to impose their morality on us. The problem with this idea is that morality, far from only concerning the individual, is primarily a relational concept, so it is found in the interactions between people. While moral relativism might sound very appealing, especially to young people today with the countless temptations they face, no one can actually live as a moral relativist. No justice system can be founded on the statement, "Don't impose your morality on me," for that is exactly what the purpose of a justice system is: to define and maintain an objective standard of morality, and to enforce it by penalizing people who fail to conform to the standard. If I'm honest with myself, I have to admit that I can't bind myself to a self-invented set of moral values and duties. When the going gets tough and a difficult moral decision is set before me, I will inevitably lower my standards and justify my actions to myself – being accountable to only yourself is like grading your own essays in college ("How about that, another A!"). This quote from Pope Emeritus Benedict XVI effectively summarizes the pitfall of moral relativism, especially in education:

> Today, a particularly insidious obstacle to the task of education is the massive presence in our society and culture of that relativism which, recognizing nothing as definitive, leaves as the ultimate criterion only the self with its desires. And under the semblance of freedom it becomes a prison for each one, for it separates people from one another, locking each person into his or her own 'ego'.

Morality is NOT a Democracy

We've seen that we can't make up morality for ourselves. But what about society? Surely whole populations of peoples can work together and agree on what is moral, then make laws that reflect those decisions and enforce the laws. This idea is known as "social contract theory," which proposes that humans choose to be moral because it is necessary in order for society to function properly. Unfortunately, we humans have a poor track record in trying to establish a social contract of morality, including the infamous and horrifying consequences of the radical ideological and political movements of the 20th century. On an even more fundamental level, can one individual make moral judgements that I am obligated to conform myself to? I think most would say, "Of course not!" The reality is, society is nothing more than a large group of individuals, and simply adding more insufficient sources of morality together does not a sufficient source make.

If one man is wrong, getting 300 million people to agree with him won't make him right – truth is qualitative, not quantitative. Since I cannot bind even myself to my own subjective standard of morality, it follows that other people cannot bind me to their standard, no matter how many of them there may be. If literally everyone in the world somehow bought into the idea that it was morally permissible to torture an innocent child for entertainment, would it then become right? What percentage of people has to agree on something before it becomes true? This is what makes utilitarianism so terrifying, because if torturing that child brought the "most happiness to the largest number of people," then we would not only be justified in doing it, we would be obligated. Clearly, what a group of people may be taught or convinced is moral cannot constitute real and objective moral values and duties. At this point, some people will cite examples of tribes of indigenous peoples who violate taboos of civilized societies, by acts such as cannibalism and human sacrifice, and claim that these examples prove that morality is nothing more than the collective creation of a given population. However, I find such examples to be exceptions that prove the rule. If an entire society can be mistaken about matters of science or mathematics, which are real and objective, then the same error is possible in matters of morality.

The House Built on Rock

So, what can the foundation of objective moral values and duties be? If it is not a product of the evolutionary process, or of personal opinion, or of social norms, or of some combination of the three, then what is it? Where does it come from? Does it even exist? The only explanation of the existence of objective moral values and duties, which are real and binding on everyone, regardless of time, place and culture, is that God created them. If God is real, and He created human beings for a purpose, namely, to conform their wills to His so that they might flourish in this life and be eventually fully united with Him in eternal life, then it makes sense that there would be a right and wrong way of going about that process of conformity, and of helping others to achieve the same end. This is the mission and purpose of the Church, not to impose her morality, but to propose Christ's, to hold him up to all people as "the way, the truth, and the life" (Jn 14:6), so that they may achieve the end for which they were created—to love and to be loved. Let us give thanks to God for revealing His perfect moral law to us, by writing it on our hearts, teaching it to us in the Sacred Scriptures, and most especially, by revealing it in its fullness through His Son, Jesus Christ, who established His Church, which is "the pillar and foundation of the truth" (1 Tim 3:15), in order that we might be guided into all truth by the Holy Spirit (Jn 16:13). Thank you for reading, and God Bless you!

† Under the Mercy,

Chris Trummer

Free Will vs. Determinism

The following post comes from the Free Will/Determinism section of the term paper for my "Human Nature and Person" class, with some modifications.

I experience myself as having the freedom to define my destiny or life course by virtue of free will. By free will, I mean the capacity of human beings to actually choose how they will think or act at any given moment. The concept of free will does not exclude influences based on the biology, environment, and circumstances of a person. Rather, it simply means that in the end, regardless of whatever various influences and pressures may be placed on a person, they are ultimately responsible for their actions. If you are tracing blame back through a causal chain of events, you can stop at each individual and not the atoms that make up their physical brain. It's interesting how impossible it is to eradicate the concept of free will from the human mind. Even the staunchest materialistic atheists cannot completely abandon the concepts implied by free will, such as credit, blame, and appreciation.

A High Price to Pay

If human beings do not have free will, then there is no justifiable reason to congratulate, thank, admire, or even punish anyone. Every justice system in history is based on the assumption that people freely choose their actions. That is why we call it "justice." Admittedly, part of the purpose of incarcerating people is to remove them from society and prevent them from harming others again. However, in court we declare those convicted to be "guilty." This is not a description of the biological, environmental, or circumstantial influences experienced by the person leading up to the crime. It is the recognition of the convicted person's free choice to commit the crime. I do not in any way wish to undermine the importance of studies within the realm of psychology and sociology, which are essential for understanding human nature better and help us to identify the ways we can improve as a society in terms of parenting, education, punishment, and rehabilitation. Rather, I'm simply arguing that it is impossible to construct and uphold a real justice system without recognizing the human capacity of free will.

On the materialist/determinist view, if someone were to (God forbid) murder your loved one, you could be angry, but it would really be pointless to say the murderer was actually to blame for it, or that he was acting immorally, because of course, his decision to commit the crime can ultimately be explained by the sum of all the physical and chemical processes occurring in his brain. These processes, while admittedly highly complex, are still completely determined by their respective physical laws. On a somewhat more positive note (no pun intended), people who hold strictly to materialism would have to agree that, from the instant that the Big Bang occurred, Johann Sebastian Bach's "St. Matthew's Passion" had to be written. This would mean that Bach did not freely respond to the creative urges in his heart, freely choose to spend countless hours practicing the organ and writing liturgical music, or even freely choose to pen any of his greatest works that bring people to tears centuries after his death. He couldn't have done anything differently then what he did. I think almost any person with a love for art and its expression would be extremely skeptical of materialism if they understood this fact.

Materialism Destroys Itself

The materialists who I've encountered fail to see just how self-refuting it is to believe in materialism. If everything you believe is reducible to chemical reactions and the movement of subatomic particles within your brain, all of which operate according to the laws of chemistry and physics, then it is meaningless to claim that one belief is "better" or more true than any other. This would of course include the belief that materialism is true. Ironically, people who believe in determinism, if they are right, are determined to believe in it! Obviously, the self-refuting nature of materialism that makes it impossible to defend does not in itself prove that materialism is false, or that humans do have free will. Moreover, if all reality was in fact completely reducible to matter and controlled only by fixed laws, then I would agree that what we perceive as free will must really be just an illusion. I've always wondered, why would a purely material process of random mutation and natural selection produce in our

14

minds the illusion of a will that was immaterial? Why would we learn to feel proud or ashamed of the way we acted, when in reality, we couldn't have acted any other way? In any case, I have not encountered any good arguments to give me reason to believe that all reality is reducible to matter. Therefore, I feel justified in holding the belief that the reason I feel so responsible for making the right choice in a given situation is because I really am responsible, because I really am free to choose.

Thanks be to God for helping us avoid the snares of dehumanizing philosophies by creating us with the ability to reason about the truth and to choose it freely. Also, for revealing the Truth in its fullness through His Son, Jesus Christ.

† Under the Mercy,

Chris Trummer

The Heavens Declare the Glory of God

"In an age of hope men looked up at the night sky and saw 'the heavens.' In an age of hopelessness they call it simply 'space.'" — Peter Kreeft

Frequently, when I'm having a conversation with someone who is either a non-believer or just having doubts, they will make an objection to religious belief that goes something like this: "Once you understand how unimaginably large the universe is, it makes you realize how insignificant we are. We humans think we're so important, but really, we're nothing in the big picture. If there was a god who cared about human beings, then he wouldn't make them such an incomprehensibly small speck in a universe that is almost completely cold, dark, and lifeless." The size of the universe use to intimidate me as well, so I can sympathize with this mentality. However, further reflection and study on this idea has settled my mind, and so I'd like to share my thoughts here.

"The Universe is Really Big" — Compared to What?

This may sound silly, but the universe (or if there is a multiverse, then the multiverse) includes everything in physical reality, so there's literally nothing else to compare it with! Size is a relational property; nothing can be described as being large or small without using something else as a reference. Have you seen other, smaller universes to know that ours is particularly large? Often the response to this objection is, "Well, it's really big compared to us." Oh, so we're the standard of size and mass that everything else should be compared with! In this case, the objector is guilty of the same human-centrism that he accuses religious people of. Also, the argument has the weakness of being based on a matter of degree. How small would the universe have to be for human beings to be significant? One-half of the size it is now? One-thousandth? One trillionth? Human beings have known for literally thousands of years that they are very small compared to the great expanse of nature around them, and this was hardly an obstacle to their believing in gods. What difference does it make to know that there are billions of galaxies out there if you already knew that you were a measly 160 pounds of flesh within an entire solar system, or even just planet Earth? The size of the Pacific Ocean alone is enough to make me feel like a grain of sand in comparison.

> When I look at your heavens, the work of your fingers, the moon and the stars which you have established; what is man that you should be mindful of him, and the son of man that you should care for him? (Psalm 8:3-4).

Size ≠ Value

The argument makes the assumption that value or significance is somehow determined by size or mass. This I find particularly strange, because in everyday life this standard is almost never used. Is 16 million pounds of scrap metal in a junk yard somehow better than a 16 million dollar fighter jet? Is a sequoia tree (the largest species of tree on the planet) more important than a cow? Is a golden retriever worth more than a seven-year-old girl? Is a mountain range more valuable than the native villagers who live at its base? Is a 40 ton boulder more significant than a human embryo? Clearly, the difference between all of these examples is one of kind and not simply degree. In other words, the difference between them is qualitative, not quantitative. When you try to compare things that are qualitatively different, there is no use in trying to multiply one to make it comparable to the other – it doesn't work. This is especially clear in the examples comparing inanimate (nonliving) matter to animate (living) matter, and those comparing unconscious living things (trees) to conscious living things (human beings). Here, the dedicated materialist will object that there really isn't any qualitative difference between, say, the boulder and the human embryo – both are only the products of the laws of nature working on matter, even if one happens to result in an evolutionary process that produces beings who are capable of a "phenomenon" where they "seem" to be conscious. I say seem because it is very common (and actually, consistent) for materialist philosophers today to deny human consciousness and thought, since they are ordinarily defined as immaterial realities, and therefore, impossible within the materialist worldview. Rather than questioning his or her own consciousness or ability to think, the person hearing claims like this should question the sanity of the person making them! However, philosophy of mind is admittedly a deep and highly complex area of study that I plan on spending more time studying and hope to write about in the future. Suffice it to say for now that, even among prominent and unbelieving philosophers, the understanding of the human mind is a highly debated and controversial subject. Take this statement from the well-established agnostic philosopher Thomas Nagel, for example:

> My guess is that [the] cosmic authority problem is not a rare condition and that it is responsible for much of the scientism and reductionism of our time. One of the tendencies it supports is the ludicrous overuse of evolutionary biology to explain everything about human life, including everything about the human mind (Nagel 130-131).

Big God, Big Universe — What's the Big Deal?

How does the creation of a (relatively) large universe count as evidence against the God of classical theism, who is understood to be infinitely powerful? The Psalmist joyfully wrote that "The heavens declare the glory of God; and the firmament (sky, expanse) proclaims his handiwork" (Ps19:1). I wonder, if the entire universe somehow consisted of only our planet and sun, would the same person not object "an all-powerful God wouldn't create a universe so small?" It seems as though God has already been ruled guilty from the outset of the trial in the objector's mind, and so now everything must count as evidence against him. The fact that the same feature of reality counts for God to the believer and against Him to the unbeliever may simply be evidence that the objections come from the disposition or desires of the objector, rather than from any actual contradiction within either the concept of God or Creation. The creation of a single atom from literally nothing is as demanding of infinite power as the creation of an entire universe, since in both cases there is, metaphysically speaking, an infinite chasm to cross – the chasm between being and non-being. The idea that the universe's largeness, emptiness, and lifelessness is evidence that humans have no value also presupposes that God is limited in His resources, an idea that no believer would agree with. In addition, the theory of evolution requires millions and millions of years in order for the planet to give rise to life and for that life to evolve. Therefore, given the laws of nature that exist, the size of universe can really be considered a necessity if life forms were intended by the Creator, since the size of the universe is a result of the amount of time it has been expanding since the Big Bang.

Mind Over Matter

Of all the trillions upon trillions of stars, planets, and other cosmic bodies in the universe, none of them is looking back at us, wondering what we are. Why does it matter if a planet is millions of times more massive than me if it is not aware of the fact? Also, if humans have immortal souls, as proposed by most major religions, than we will continue to exist after the entire universe reaches "heat death," the complete reduction of all ordered systems to a state of disordered equilibrium, as dictated by the law of entropy. True meaning or significance can only exist in something eternal. Why? If something existed for a time, and then ceased to exist, and eventually all of its effects ceased to exist, then we would say that thing has literally no meaning. Actually, we wouldn't say anything about it, because we would have no way of even knowing that it had no meaning. The same could be said about the universe its self:

> If the whole universe has no meaning, we should never have found out
> that it has no meaning: just as, if there were no light in the universe and
> therefore no creatures with eyes, we should never know it was dark. Dark
> would be without meaning. — C.S. Lewis

Say there was a book written by a man who lived in a small village. One day this book was destroyed in a fire, and the man who wrote it later died, and then eventually all of his friends, family, and fellow villagers who knew about him and his book died, and every single piece of evidence that the book ever even existed was destroyed. It would then be impossible to say that what had been contained in that book had "meaning." No quark, atom, molecule, rock, planet, tree, or even animal can ever be the subject in a sentence, can ever say the word, "I." This reality of the self, which has been the most puzzling fact since the dawn of human thought, is what

20

makes us worth more than an entire universe of inanimate matter. I give thanks to God my Creator for giving me my very self, which is not reducible to matter, and therefore worth more than all the matter in the cosmos combined, even if there is more of it than I can wrap my mind around. Thank you for reading, and God Bless you!

† Under the Mercy,

Chris Trummer

Sources:

Catholic Biblical Association (Great Britain). *The Holy Bible: Revised Standard Version, Catholic Edition*. New York: National Council of Churches of Christ in the USA, 1994. Print.

Lewis, C.S.. *Mere Christianity*. Harper: San Francisco, 2009. Print.

Nagel, Thomas. *The Last Word*. Oxford University Press, 1997. pp. 130-131.

How Will You Wager? A Closer Look at Pascal's Famous Argument

In our lives, we have to make decisions constantly. These range from small, relatively unimportant decisions like choosing between Coke and Pepsi, to critical life decisions like the choice between going to college or heading straight into the workforce, marrying or remaining single, and one side of a moral debate and the other. One decision that is more important than any other by its very nature is the decision of whether or not to believe in God. I say "by its very nature" because the decision has eternal repercussions.

From France With Wisdom

One of my favorite books is *Christianity for Modern Pagans* by Peter Kreeft, which deals with this most important decision by outlining and explaining the *Pensées* (Thoughts), by Blaise Pascal. Pascal was a French-Catholic philosopher, scientist, and apologist who lived during the 17th century. He was a contemporary of Descartes, and until the 19th century was the only philosopher who didn't jump on the ideological bandwagon misnamed the "Enlightenment." Contrary to common misconception, he was not a Jansenist (the heretical group condemned by the Church during his time), at least in terms of his own theology, although he was associated with Jansenists. He was, however, a great physicist, mathematician, and inventor; he invented the first working computer (the Pascaline, a mechanical calculator), vacuum cleaner, and public transportation system. In the area of philosophy, Pascal is best known for his "Wager," which is an argument for the reasonableness of believing in God. The argument is not in any way a proof for God's existence; it is more of a thought experiment that approaches belief in God by a cost-to-reward analysis. Many philosophers and theologians throughout history have believed that the existence of God can be proven with varying degrees of certainty. For the sake of the Wager, Pascal assumes that you cannot prove the existence of God by reason alone, using philosophical arguments. Pascal instead wants you to consider what you can gain or lose by choosing to believe in God or not.

Belief is a wise wager. Granted that faith cannot be proved, what harm will come to you if you gamble on its truth and it proves false? If you gain, you gain all; if you lose, you lose nothing. Wager, then, without hesitation, that He exists.

Not Wagering is Not an Option

Many people are turned off by the idea of "betting" about God's existence. Isn't is selfish and low to believe in God "just in case" He exists so that you can go to heaven (or not go to hell)? Of course it is! Okay, then wouldn't it be better to just remain an honest agnostic? No. Why not? Why not just choose to not wager at all? "...you must wager," says Pascal, "There is no choice, you are already committed." All of us are like ships embarked on a journey. We see a port through the fog, and we have the choice of putting in to that port or not. Eventually though, the ship will run out of fuel, and the opportunity to put in to the port will be lost. Intellectually, it is possible to be agnostic, to say, "I don't know whether or not God exists." However, it is impossible to actually live as an agnostic (I know from experience)—you're either going to live as if God exists or as if He doesn't exist.

Love Stoops to Conquer

The Wager does presuppose some things. For example, it assumes that belief in God is necessary for salvation. However, this assumption is a basic tenet in most major religions, and there are very good theological reasons for believing it. Any religious ideology that includes both salvation and free will must also include the possibility of damnation (For more on this topic, see my post, "A Door Locked from the Inside"). Furthermore, Pascal never claims that the belief resulting from a selfishly made "bet" on God's existence is in any way sufficient for salvation. However, God is not a cosmic dictator; He is more like a lover, and love stoops to conquer. God will accept the less than ideal motivations a person has for believing in Him at the start of their journey, but that doesn't mean that He will be satisfied with them. In the book *Christianity for Modern*

24

Pagans, Peter Kreeft offers a beautiful analogy for this. He says that God is like a parent watching their child learn to walk—pleased and filled with joy at the toddler's first clumsy steps, but not totally satisfied until the child is running around the yard with other children. God loves us the way we are, but he loves us too much to leave us that way.

Motivation—Not Proof

The Wager cannot convince a person that God exists (it isn't intended to), but it can convince them that indifference and agnosticism are not reasonable options. There is an epidemic of apathy in our world today, especially in our country. Apathy is like an infection that is resistant to all antibiotics, the antibiotics being rational argument, and the person's appetite for the truth is like their own immune system—both together work to kill the infection. Upon hearing about Pascal's Wager, many skeptics object: "I won't believe in something just because I can gain something if it turns out to be true. If God exists, knows everything, and wants me to believe in Him, then He knows exactly what it would take for me to believe. Since I don't believe, God must either not exist or not care enough to reveal Himself to me. In either case, why believe in Him?"

Seek and You Shall Find

I am completely sympathetic with the skeptic's objection. The only reason that anyone should ever believe anything at all is because it is true. However, I disagree with the skeptic is in his assumption that God has not already done what is necessary to convince him to believe. Jesus says, "Seek, and you shall find" and through the prophet Jeremiah, God said, "You will seek me and find me; when you seek me with all your heart" (Jer. 29:13). When you seek me with all your heart. The question is, are you really seeking God with all your heart? Are you really laying down your weapons—surrendering your passions and opening your heart and mind to the possibility that God is real and He loves you, or are you arbitrarily setting your criteria for belief at a level which you know that God probably will never accommodate, so that you can fool yourself into thinking your unbelief is justified? "Unless x, y, or z happened, then I will not believe in God." When a person sets an ultimatum in this way, they are demanding that God overwhelm their decision to live apart from Him. God cannot do this without undermining the person's free will. "In faith there is enough light for those who want to believe and enough shadows to blind those who don't" (Pensées).

Pascal divides people into three groups: Those who have sought God and have found Him, those who are seeking God and have not yet found Him, and those who neither seek God nor find Him. Those in the first group are reasonable because they have sought, and happy because they have found; those in the second group are reasonable because they are seeking, but unhappy because they have not yet found; those in the third group are neither reasonable nor happy, because they are not seeking and so they have not (and cannot) find. Notice that there is no fourth group consisting of people who find without seeking. If you decide that you don't want to know or love God, He will not override your decision—God is a lover, not a rapist. He invites, He doesn't coerce. When two of John the Baptist's disciples asked Jesus where He was staying, He replied, "Come and see" (Jn 1:39). If you've already made up your mind that the Christian God is unreasonable, oppressive, childish, or even just too good to be true, and that nothing will convince you otherwise, then you can rest assured that God will leave you alone.

Momento Mori (Remember Death)

We all have a terminal illness called mortality. Every second that passes brings us closer to that moment when we will face our death. To live in a way that ignores this fact is seriously delusional, which is why atheists who seem happy and content with facing their death are in such a dangerous position. God "desires all men to be saved and to come to the knowledge of the truth" (1 Tim. 2:4) but if your heart is set against God and the truth, then there is no way for Divine Mercy to reach you. That is why it is so important that we pray for all those who do not believe in God, and especially those who do not even seek Him. I hope you will join me in this prayer, and thank you for reading! God Bless!

26

† Under the Mercy,

Chris Trummer

Sources:

Catholic Biblical Association (Great Britain). The Holy Bible: Revised Standard Version, Catholic Edition. New York: National Council of Churches of Christ in the USA, 1994. Print.

Hell: A Door Locked from the Inside

"I can't believe that a loving God would send people to hell."

"Why did God create some people if He knew they would reject Him and go to hell?"

"If God is all-powerful and all-good, then why doesn't He just destroy Satan and hell?"

"As long as you're a decent person then there's no way you'll end up in hell."

"Hell is just something the Church made up to scare people into behaving well."

"Hell might exist, but there probably isn't anyone there."

These are objections that I encounter all the time, and ones that are extremely common among non-believers, non-Christians, and even Christians. The objections are honest and fair for the most part, because the Christian concept of hell can be confusing and even seem contradictory to the Gospel message if one doesn't understand it properly. In this post, I intend to show that the Christian doctrine of hell is:

1. Logically necessary.
2. Consistent with Christ's message of love, forgiveness, and mercy.
3. Widely misunderstood by both Christians and non-Christians today.

Love Requires Freedom

First, what do I mean when I say that the doctrine of hell is necessary? It's necessary because it is impossible for God to be loving without the existence of hell. Whoa, that sounds like a bold claim—why do you say that? I'll tell you. Christians believe that God created human beings with free will, meaning that they are free to choose what and whom they will love, and what and whom they will reject. If you reject someone, do you want to spend time with them or get to know them better? Certainly not. This freedom applies to God as well. God will not force anyone to accept and love Him. In fact, He can't force anyone to love Him, because love has to be a free choice by definition. "Forced love" is like a "square circle." If Heaven is God's love and presence for eternity, then how could anyone who rejected God be happy there? This is where the issue of free will arises. If a person dies in a state where they completely reject God and want nothing to do with His love or forgiveness, would it be loving for God to bring them to Heaven anyway? God would effectively be saying, "I know you won't love me but since I'm all-powerful and I know what's best for you, I'm going to force you to love me." Thats' not love, but tyranny, and God is not a tyrant! Demanding that God bring everyone to heaven, with or without their consent, is like a bride reciting her vows because the groom is holding a gun to her head. In *The Problem of Pain*, C.S. Lewis asks a question that cuts to the heart of this objection:

> What are you asking God to do?' To wipe out their past sins and, at all costs, to give them a fresh start, smoothing every difficulty and offering every miraculous help? But He has done so, on Calvary. To forgive them? They will not be forgiven. To leave them alone? Alas, I am afraid that is what He does. (Lewis 128).

The Problem With Universal Salvation

There is a theory with growing popularity, sometimes referred to as "universal salvation," which attempts to avoid the problem of hell by suggesting that upon death, God reveals Himself to the unrepentant sinner, who is so overwhelmed by God's Truth, Beauty, and Goodness that he cannot help but to love God and repent of his sins. This idea might sound comforting or reassuring at first, but take a closer look at it. If God were going to overwhelm every hell-destined person at the end of their life, so that they could be forgiven and be with Him in Heaven, then how would that affect the meaning of that person's life on Earth? It would render it meaningless. Why? Take this example. Let's say you've made no effort during your life to seek God, to know, love, or serve Him, but instead you've actively rejected Him in all your thoughts, words, and actions. Eventually, one day you die, still obstinately refusing God's love. If God would, at that moment of your death, reveal Himself in such a way that you literally had no choice but to love Him and beg for forgiveness and mercy, then He would in doing so eliminate the meaning of every choice you ever made. If nothing you think, say, or do can ever override God's "overwhelming" effect on you at death, then no set of beliefs or way of living can be considered ultimately better than any other, since each produces the same effect—salvation. This raises another problem, related to the problem of suffering. If God was planning on overwhelming even the most evil people into loving Him at the end of their lives, then why didn't He reveal himself to them before they hurt, misled, corrupted, and even killed countless innocent people? If God could have simply "overwhelmed" Hitler into loving Him, then why didn't He do so before the horrors of Holocaust? The truth is, if God could somehow force people to accept Him, then waiting to do so until after those people spend their entire lives inflicting pain and suffering on others would be heartless indifference at best, and cruelty at worst.

The Hard Way and the Narrow Gate

I said that the doctrine of hell is perfectly consistent with Christ's message of love, forgiveness, and mercy. Many people who are not familiar with the Bible assume that most of the "hell stuff" must come from the Old Testament, which was of course all about the God of divine wrath, justice, and fury, right? Wrong! In fact, the vast majority of what we know about hell comes from Jesus Christ himself! If hell does not exist, or is at least nothing for us to worry about, then Jesus was either seriously confused or purposely trying to deceive people. Jesus tells us to enter through the narrow gate by the hard way and that "the way is easy that leads to destruction" (Mt 7:13-14). If everyone is eventually saved, regardless of whether they want to be or not, then Jesus' analogy of the "narrow gate" is a completely unnecessary warning. How could the gate that everyone passes through be described as "narrow," and the way that leads to it as "hard"? (That doesn't sound so hard to me!) Just a couple paragraphs later in Matthew's gospel, we hear what Jesus' response will be to those who plead with him during their judgement, after never trying to do his Father's will during their lives:

> "Not every one who says to me, 'Lord, Lord,' shall enter the kingdom of
> heaven, but he who does the will of my Father who is in heaven. On that
> day many will say to me, 'Lord, Lord, did we not prophesy in your name,

and cast out demons in your name, and do many mighty works in your name?' And then will I declare to them, 'I never knew you; depart from me, you evildoers' (Mt 7:21-23).

Hell is Ultimately a Choice

I never knew you. These are the words that some people describe as the saddest words in the bible. They give me the chills, because they capture that horrifying moment when a person finally realizes that the time for turning back is over, and that death has transformed their temporary response of "Maybe God" or "Not yet God" into a permanent "No God." So how is all this exclusion and damnation consistent with Christ's message of love, forgiveness, and mercy? All three of these Divine gifts have to be accepted. Loving God is meaningless without the option of hating him, receiving forgiveness is meaningless without the option of refusing it, and God's mercy is meaningless without his justice. Without the freedom to be a Hitler, there is nothing great or admirable about being a Mother Teresa. This fact, that going to hell is ultimately a free choice, is why C.S. Lewis described hell as "a door locked from the inside." While the people in hell are certainly not happy to be there, and obviously can't enjoy the suffering of being eternally separated from God, they would be even more miserable to be in God's presence in Heaven. This is difficult to understand, like trying to understand a person's decision to end their own life—it breaks our hearts and boggles our minds. However, the difficulty we have in trying to understand it and the heartbreak that it makes us feel is surely a positive sign, one that shows we are still striving to know and love God more ourselves. Some people reject the idea that going to hell is ultimately a choice, and instead insist on the idea that hell is some kind of eternal torture chamber where people are sent against their will. This mentality seems to arise from an emotional or even revengeful response to the sin and injustice in the world. However, we cannot possibly know the dispositions or motivations of other people, regardless of how immoral their conduct may seem, and it is certainly neither our right nor to our benefit to fantasize about what punishment we feel must be necessary to satisfy God's justice.

Why the Downplaying of Hell?

The abundance of Christians today who seriously downplay or even deny the doctrine of hell is evidence that the doctrine is greatly misunderstood. I believe that the three greatest contributors to this widespread misunderstanding are:

1. An overly-literal interpretation of the imagery of hell found in Scripture.
2. The comical or childish portrayal of hell and final judgement in modern literature, television shows, and film.
3. A lack of good catechesis and preaching on the doctrine of hell during the last fifty or sixty years.

Who is Satan?

I won't go into depth on each of these issues now, because a book could be written on each, and I suspect (and hope) that most people are probably already aware of their influence to some extent. I will mention one especially common misunderstanding though, the identity of Satan. Many people seem to understand Satan as being God's arch nemesis, as Lex Luthor is to Superman. This is totally inaccurate, because is gives the impression that Satan is in some way on the same level as God, which is absurd. Satan is an angel, a spiritual being created by God, who rejected God because of his pride and so was cast out of God's presence. He was once known as Lucifer (light-bearer), and was the greatest among the *Seraphim*, the highest choir in the hierarchy of angels. The Hebrew word *seraphim* literally translates to "burning ones," because the Seraphs are so close to God that they are constantly on fire with His love. Since Lucifer was the highest in heaven (among the created beings), and chose to turn away from God, his fall from Grace was the greatest fall possible. As the saying goes, "The bigger they are, the harder they fall." Satan is therefore not some creepy guy in red tights with horns and a trident whom God has raised to the rank of "torture master." He does not "reign" in hell—he is the lowest, most pitiable, and most miserable one, because he has lost more than anyone else who might be there. At best one could say that he is the chief rebel. God is uncreated and infinite and Satan created and finite. To God, Satan's rebellion is like a three year-old having a tantrum and hitting Daddy, except Satan is even less of a threat. Of course, I use this analogy to describe the relationship between God and Satan—not the relationship between Satan and other created beings, like us, among whom he still has great power and influence.

In conclusion, I hope my thoughts on this crucial doctrine have shed some light on it and sparked interest for further reading. Speaking of further reading, it would be a great disservice to the reader if I did not recommend reading C.S. Lewis' book *The Problem of Pain*, or at least the eighth chapter, which is on hell. Also, I highly, highly recommend *The Handbook of Catholic Apologetics*, written by Dr. Peter Kreeft and Fr. Ronald Tacelli, S.J., not only for its chapter on hell (Chapter 12), but because it is in my opinion a must-have for all Catholics. God bless you, and thanks for reading!

† Under the Mercy,

Chris Trummer

Sources:

Catholic Biblical Association (Great Britain). *The Holy Bible: Revised Standard Version, Catholic Edition*. New York: National Council of Churches of Christ in the USA, 1994. Print.

Lewis, C.S. *The Problem of Pain*. 1940.

Sometimes Quiet is Violent: Finding Silence in a World Full of Noise

From time to time, we all find ourselves pondering the deepest questions in life, ones about what the Catholic apologist Matt Fradd refers to as G.L.U.E. (God, Life, the Universe, and Everything). Some people just call them "the biggies." These questions include: "What is the meaning of my life? Is there a reason for my existence? Does God exist? What happens when we die, if anything?" When asked for his opinion on questions like these in an interview, the atheist Richard Dawkins responded, "The 'why' questions are the silly questions." It's interesting how the questions we have most wanted answered throughout human history, the questions that have provoked in us the most wonder and deep thought are the "silly" questions. This is one of the tragedies of atheism—it forces you to abandon the hope that questions about ultimate meaning or purpose will ever be answered.

Just a few years ago, while I didn't consider these questions "silly", I feared them like a cancer diagnosis. In our society, we have a prevailing tendency to engage in small talk, to busy ourselves with lots of little things, and to fill every free moment with some form of entertainment, stimulation, or just plain noise. This is telling of just how afraid we are to face these most important questions. Blaise Pascal once wrote, "All of man's problems come from his inability to sit quietly in a room by himself." Is that really true? It certainly sounds a little extreme, yet there is great wisdom in it. When Pascal says that our problems "come from" this inability, he means that the inability shows we are guilty of not being able to face our own mortality. Perhaps you're thinking to yourself right now, "I'm not addicted to distractions or afraid to face the big questions in life. I don't mind sitting quietly by myself either." If you are thinking this, I have a challenge for you. *Try it.* Try actually sitting in a room alone without your phone, lights, music, or any other source of noise for half an hour. You'll probably find that it's not nearly as easy as it sounds. If this does sound too difficult, try just turning off your car radio the next time you make a half-hour drive by yourself. Ironically, there is a song called "Car Radio" by the band Twenty One Pilots that illustrates our addiction to distracting ourselves in a very powerful way. The philosopher Soren

Kierkegaard was very much aware of the human aversion to silence, even though he lived before the age of radio, cable television, the Internet, YouTube, Netflix, and all the other technological distractions that we have today. He once wrote:

> If I were a physician, and if I were allowed to prescribe just one remedy for all the ills of the modern world, I would prescribe silence. For even if the Word of God were proclaimed in the modern world, no one would hear it; there is too much noise. Therefore, create silence.

Do you know anyone who constantly looks at their phone when you're trying to talk to them? They might nod occasionally, saying "Yeah...yeah...I know what you mean," but they clearing aren't paying attention. If you're able to read this blog right now, then I'm sure you have experienced this, and you know how frustrating it can be. When it comes to our relationship with God, we are too often that annoying friend on our phone. We rightly expect our fellow human beings to give us their full attention when we speak to them, but when we supposedly want to listen to our Creator and the Creator of the entire universe, we rarely give the same consideration to Him. Some people even do this intentionally, rationalizing their lack of effort to hear God, thinking that "If God really wanted to speak to me, then He could make Himself heard; He could drown out whatever noise there is in my life." This is a dangerous attitude to have, because it is rooted in pride and basically amounts to telling God, "God, I want to listen to you but I'm only willing to do so on my terms." If you refuse to approach God just because the way He ordinarily communicates with people doesn't completely make sense to you, then you're not even giving Him a chance. God is a package deal, like a spouse. When you marry someone, your life should now be lived for your spouse, and your spouse's life likewise be lived for you. If you wish to enter into marriage with a person, but are unwilling to change anything about yourself, your priorities, or how you spend your time, then you can't expect that relationship to be healthy or your marriage to last. The same goes for your relationship with God.

Religion is not a Do-it-Yourself project, in which having a relationship with God is some sort of quantifiable, calculable state that can be achieved by simply taking the proper steps and following the instructions. A relationship is not merely the results of some properly observed method. God is a *personal* being, and we should approach Him that way. This is why prayer is absolutely essential. If you love someone, you want to get to know them, if you want to get know them, you have to communicate with them, and to communicate with them you have to give them your time and undivided attention. How do we apply this practically to our relationship with God? A good place to start is to find some silence each day, and give our over-stimulated minds a break from the endless flood of noise that our technological age bombards us with. This might mean setting your alarm ten or fifteen minutes earlier (gasp!) so that you can start your day off with some Bible or other book reading, quiet meditation, a rosary, or other favorite prayer of yours. I can personally guarantee that you'll be surprised at how much your mood, attitude, and most importantly, spiritual well-being will benefit by offering God the first fruits of your day. "But Chris, I'm NOT a morning person, and what little time I do have is spent rushing around getting myself ready, my kids ready, my spouse ready, my dog ready, etc." I completely understand. What time of day are you at your best then? On your lunch break? During the afternoon? The evening? At one o'clock in the morning, when you're usually still on Facebook? Regardless of what time you're available, we all can afford to give God fifteen minutes of our best time. Too often, we put off our time with God until "When I get extra time." Let's face it, something else will come up, or you'll forget, so the time for God is going to have come from what most of us call "my" time. Of course, the concept of *my* time is merely a delusion, because every second of our existence is a free gift from God! One final and easy way to introduce healthy silence into your day is to simply turn off your car radio the next time you're driving and "just sit in silence." If you feel like you can't part with your driving tunes, carefully listen to and/or read the lyrics of the song "Car Radio" and reflect on what it may be that you're hiding from, or rather, *Who* it may be you're hiding from, when you bury yourself in noise.

† Under the Mercy,

Chris Trummer

The Failed Experiment: Finding Happiness Apart from God

"We are at the end of a tradition and a civilization which believed we could preserve Christianity without Christ, religion without a creed, meditation without sacrifice, family life without moral responsibility, sex without purity and economics without ethics. We have completed our experiment of living without God." — Venerable Fulton J. Sheen

In a way, all of us are like scientists. Our goal is to define, understand, and finally secure happiness in life. Our lives are a continual process of experimentation; we form hypotheses about what we think will make us happy, and then we test the hypotheses. Our laboratory is the entire world, and we have a wide variety of tools and instruments at our disposal. There is great disagreement about which tools we should use, which methods we should employ, which hypothesis is correct, and how we should measure the success of our experiment. The only thing that we all agree on is the goal of the experiment, happiness. Can you imagine any other motive for doing something besides thinking that it will make you happy? It's impossible – every good thing we can obtain or experience in life is considered good to the extent that it produces happiness. We're familiar with the question, "What good are riches if they don't make you happy?" and, "Money can't buy you happiness." Conversely, nobody asks, "What good is happiness if it doesn't make you rich?" This fact, that happiness is the end (purpose) of human life, is so deeply engrained in human nature that it seems unnecessary to even point it out. And yet, acknowledging it is the first step in evaluating the choices we make in life.

When Fulton Sheen said that "we have completed our experiment of living without God," he didn't mean that we aren't still repeating the experiment, after all, he said that in 1933, and look how much further our culture has regressed since then! Rather, he meant that we are fully aware of the results of our experiment—total failure. Every time we try to root our happiness in something less than God, we are left disappointed. "If I just made this much more money a year, if I could just afford this outfit, this phone, this car, this house; if I could just get this person to notice me, this person to like me, and this person to respect me; if I could just change this one thing about myself, this one thing about my spouse . . . then I would be happy." Sound familiar? We all tell ourselves these things from time to time. However, I believe that, in our deepest self, we all know they're not true. How do we know? Personal experience, along with the witness of the thousands of lives we encounter. Regardless of whether or not Einstein actually said it, we're all familiar with the quote, "Insanity is doing the same thing over and over and expecting different results." There is also the similar, "If you do what you've always done, you'll get what you've always got." Everyone agrees with these ideas, so what does this mean? We're insane! Perhaps not logically insane, but at least practically insane. Peter Kreeft says that this insanity of ours is for him a proof of the Fall and Original Sin. Saint Paul was perplexed by this insanity in himself, which he writes about in his letter to the Romans: "I do not understand my own actions. For I do not do what I want, but I do the very thing I hate...I do not do the good I want, but the evil I do not want is what I do" (Romans 7:15,19).

Take a moment to reflect on a time when you managed to forget yourself and live completely for someone else, whether it was listening to a friend who was struggling with something, or volunteering as part of a charitable outreach, or just doing a random act of kindness. Remember how liberating and satisfying that felt? Now think of what is probably (if you're anything like me) the more common reality, the times when you've been completely selfish, when you've made a decision based solely on the consideration of "What's in it for me?" How did that make you feel, and how did that feeling compare with what you felt in the first scenario? In my experience, selflessness has always brought me authentic, lasting happiness, while selfishness has given me only disappointment, dissatisfaction, and frustration. I've observed the same results in the life of every single person I've ever met. And yet, fully aware of what works and what doesn't, we deceive ourselves so that we can perform the experiment "one more time." And the cycle repeats...

But wait, what happened to "survival of the fittest?" Why do the qualities and virtues that we admire the most in others, and strive hardest to possess ourselves (humility, self-sacrifice, altruism, etc.) seem to be in direct opposition to the ones that provide us with the best chances for survival and flourishing on a biological level (pride, selfishness, and domination)? Why does human nature seem more excellent to us the further it diverges from the route of personal advantage? Why do non-Christians and even many secular people find Christ's teachings so true, good, and beautiful, when He so blatantly contradicts everything our culture tells us we need to be happy? Why do we admire the saints so much if most of them were, by every worldly standard, failures? I think all of these questions have one answer – our happiness lies in God alone. Why do we repeat the failed experiment? Saint Augustine found the answer: "You have made us for yourself, and our hearts are restless until they rest in you" (*Confessions*)

If you feel restless, anxious, scared, discontent, dissatisfied, broken, or unworthy, or all of the above, know that you don't have to keep wandering around in a hopeless search for happiness. Happiness is waiting for you, and He has a name—Jesus Christ. He is more willing to forgive you than you are to ask for His forgiveness, and more willing to find you than you are to be found by Him. He knows you more than you know yourself, and He loves you more than you love yourself. He is waiting patiently: "Behold, I stand at the door and knock; if any one hears my voice and opens the door, I will come in to him and eat with him, and he with me" (Rev. 3:20).

You have to answer the door yourself, no one else can answer the door of your soul for you, and Christ isn't going to kick it down. He's not the policeman bashing on your door, He's the lover who throws pebbles at your window.

Thank you for reading and God Bless!

† Under the Mercy,

Chris Trummer

This is a Hard Saying, Who Can Listen to It?

> "I am the living bread which came down from heaven; if any one eats of this bread, he will live for ever; and the bread which I shall give for the life of the world is my flesh...he who eats my flesh and drinks my blood has eternal life, and I will raise him up at the last day." ...Many of his disciples, when they heard it, said, "This is a hard saying; who can listen to it?"

The Catholic Church not only "listens to" this saying of Jesus, but unapologetically and joyfully proclaims it. The Eucharist is without a doubt one of the biggest, if not the biggest stumbling block for people who would otherwise be open to the Catholic Faith. And yet, it is described by the Church as, "...the source and summit of the Christian life" (*Lumen Gentium* 11). Indeed, far from being some side issue, "small potatoes," or simply another part of the "package deal" of being Catholic, the Eucharist is (or if not, should be!) at the very core of our theology, liturgy, prayer, and worship. Sadly, despite the centrality of the Eucharist in Catholic worship and teaching, several recent surveys have revealed that an increasing number of Catholics don't believe in the Real Presence of Christ in the Eucharist, and in fact, many aren't even aware that the Church teaches it! As someone who has had his faith revitalized, largely due to accepting and embracing the reality of the Eucharist, I find this disheartening. Fortunately, the Church is very much aware of this decline in belief of one of her most central doctrines, and countless Catholics today, both clergy and laity, are doing outstanding work to restore the Eucharist to its rightful place as "source and summit" in the lives of Catholics around the world.

This Saying is Hard

If you're Catholic, and you claim that you have no difficulty whatsoever in believing the doctrine of the Real Presence, then there's a good chance you haven't yet deeply reflected on what you're saying "Amen" to at the front of the Communion line at Mass. When the priest presents the Host to you and says, "The Body of Christ," and you respond, "Amen," you are literally saying you believe that the Second Person of the Holy Trinity, the Eternal Word by whom the entire universe was created out of nothing, is being placed on your tongue and sliding down your throat into your stomach. If you take a moment to step back and consider how insane that sounds, you can better sympathize with Protestants and other non-Catholics who reject what the Church teaches about the Eucharist. I can think of only three possible explanations for a person having no doubts or difficulties accepting the Real Presence of Christ in the Eucharist: 1) an ignorance of what the Church actually teaches about the Eucharist, namely, that the bread and wine are substantially changed into the body, blood, soul and divinity of Jesus Christ, 2) a false sense of piety that is really laziness, and allows one to blindly accept what one is told without any attempt to personally understand it, or 3) a special grace from God, most likely granted in response to much humble prayer and contemplation.

So then, what if Catholics are wrong? What if the Eucharist was intended by Christ to be only a symbol of his body and blood? What if it was his body and blood, but it was only a one-time deal, and The Last Supper really was The Last Supper? Hasn't modern science disproved an idea as anti-scientific as the Eucharist?

The Eucharist is NOT Merely a Symbol

One starting piece of evidence for understanding the literal nature of the Eucharist comes from The Last Supper. If Jesus was only speaking symbolically when he said that his body would be bread given up for us, then why did he pick up an actual piece of bread and say, "This is my body" (Mt: 26:26)? At this point in the discussion, many Protestants will point out that, elsewhere in the Gospels, Jesus tells people that he is "the gate," "the vine," "the light of the world," and "the shepherd." There is an important distinction to make between these claims of Christ and the claim he made about the Eucharist. Jesus didn't hold up a gate or a vine and say, "This is my body." Obviously, Jesus wasn't literally (i.e. physically) any of those things – they are symbols he used to teach us about his relationship with us. Couldn't the Eucharist be like these then, another symbol used to remind us that Christ nourishes us and is always present among us?

Indeed it can be, and it is, but it's a mistake to think that it is *only* that. To put it plainly, if Jesus intended the Eucharist to serve as just a symbol of his body and blood, then *nobody* got the message. This is evident in the reactions of the people in the story, which ranged from confusion and disgust to trusting acceptance. The Jews were clearly scandalized and said, "How can this man give us his flesh to eat?" (Jn 6:52), many of his disciples said, "This is a hard saying, who can listen to it?" (v. 60) and they no longer followed Jesus (v. 66). Question: Is it a hard saying if Jesus is speaking symbolically? No, not really. It surely wouldn't have been hard enough that the same people who were willing to leave behind their families, friends, homes, and jobs just to follow Jesus would walk away when they heard it. After all, many of these people were probably present when Jesus said he was "the gate" and "the vine," and they handled that pretty well, because they knew he wasn't speaking literally in those cases.

If Jesus wanted to reassure everyone that he was only speaking symbolically, or at least tone down his language a bit, then he had plenty of opportunities to do so. Instead of doing this, or letting his apostles know what he "really" meant, like he did in the past when he explained parables to them, he gives them an ultimatum, putting them on the spot in front of everybody: "Do you also wish to go away?" (v. 68). Peter, speaking on behalf of all the apostles, responded, "Lord, to whom shall we go? You have the words of eternal life; and we have believed, and have come to know, that you are the Holy One of God" (v. 68-69). Here Peter was effectively saying, "Well, we don't understand exactly how this is possible, but we know you Jesus, and so we know that we can trust what you say." Had Jesus not waited until near the end of ministry to teach his apostles about the Eucharist, until after they had developed a relationship with him, they probably would have walked away with the others. Later, Jesus would say to Peter, "Feed my sheep" (Mt 21:17). Feed them what, Jesus? "The bread which I shall give for the life of the world," my flesh, which is "food indeed," and my blood, which is "drink indeed" (Jn 6:55).

Were the apostles just an anomaly though, the only ones who both took Jesus literally and believed him, perhaps out of some sense of fanatical discipleship? Not hardly. If Jesus wasn't speaking literally about the Eucharist, then Saint Paul, a convert who had severely persecuted Christians, was also very confused. When writing to the Corinthians about the Eucharist, he begins by asserting that what he is teaching is not his own invention, but was given to him directly by Christ: "For I received from the Lord what I also delivered to you (1 Cor 11:23). He goes on to make a series of bold statements: "Whoever, therefore, eats the bread or drinks the cup of the Lord in an unworthy manner will be guilty of profaning the body and blood of the Lord" (11:27).

Guilty of profaning the body and blood of the Lord. Wow, don't you think that language is a bit strong, Paul? What did he mean by this? Consider this analogy: If I were to take a gun and shoot a picture of your grandmother, that would be disrespectful, right? Right, but I wouldn't be guilty of homicide, because the picture is merely a representation or symbol of your grandmother—it's not her actually body. The same logic applies to the Eucharist. If the bread and wine are only symbols of Christ's body and blood, then while it would certainly be inappropriate to disrespect them, you couldn't be considered guilty of Christ's actual body and blood. Furthermore, why does one need to be "worthy" to receive a symbol or representation? Saint Paul speaks more about this as he continues:

> Let a man examine himself, and so eat of the bread and drink of the cup. For any one who eats and drinks without discerning the body eats and drinks judgment upon himself. That is why many of you are weak and ill, and some have died (11:28-30).

More strong language here: Discern the body, or you will eat and drink judgement upon yourself, get sick, and possibly even die (yikes!). The word "discern" means "to perceive or recognize something by the senses or by the intellect." Given the physical appearances and properties of bread and wine, which remain after Consecration, we cannot perceive the Real Presence with our human senses. However, this fact alone does not justify skepticism towards the Eucharist, because you couldn't physically see or sense Christ's divinity when he was on Earth either! Therefore, the skepticism that rejects the Eucharist is the same breed of skepticism that rejects the Incarnation. Both the Incarnation and the Eucharist are unexpected and even seem counterintuitive, or at least too good to be true. That is why they must be spiritually discerned to be believed, which is

46

probably what Jesus meant when he followed up his teaching on the Eucharist by saying, "It is the spirit that gives life, the flesh is of no avail; the words that I have spoken to you are spirit and life" (Jn 6:63). You cannot ascent to the Truth of the Real Presence by worldly reasoning. Saint Paul explained this concept to the Corinthians: "The unspiritual man does not receive the gifts of the Spirit of God, for they are folly to him, and he is not able to understand them because they are spiritually discerned" (1 Cor 2:14).

When reading any story in the Bible, it is useful to imagine where we fit into the story. For example, in the parable of the Prodigal or Lost Son, I identify most with the lost son, who rejected his father but later returned and received unconditional love, forgiveness, and mercy. In this account of Jesus' teaching about the Eucharist, ask yourself this: "Where am I in the story? Am I with Peter and the other apostles? Or am I with those who walked away from Jesus, who 'drew back and no longer went about with him?'" (Jn 6:66). To whom will *YOU* go?

The Eucharist is an Ongoing Reality

"I am the living bread which came down from heaven; if any one eats of this bread, he will live for ever; and the bread which I shall give for the life of the world is my flesh" (Jn 6:51). In this passage, notice how Jesus uses both past and future tense verbs: *I am the living bread which came down* [past tense] *from heaven* and *the bread which I shall give* [future tense] *for the life of the world is my flesh.* As Christians, we believe that Jesus has always been God, but that he came into Creation by the Incarnation at a specific time in history, making it a past event (not his being Incarnate, but the actual moment he was conceived). So, what about the future tense here? What did Jesus mean when he said "the bread which I *shall* give"? Some will say that perhaps Jesus was using an analogy here, referring to how he would give his body (the bread) to us by his dying on the cross for our sake. This is certainly true in one sense, but is that all that he meant by it? It can't be, because at the Last Supper he commanded his apostles, "Do this in memory of me" (1 Cor 11:24) meaning that what he was giving them was to be repeated in the future, which is exactly what a Catholic priest does every time he celebrates the Mass.

Don't Try to Fit the Eucharist into Your Box

Some Catholics, who I'm naturally inclined to agree with, think that we should point skeptics to the countless, well-documented Eucharistic miracles as proof of the Real Presence. While some people, if they are especially open-minded, may be swayed by the evidence of historical and ongoing Eucharistic miracles, and a select few even convinced by it, this strategy usually isn't very effective. Why not? It certainly seems like it should work: "Don't believe in the Real Presence? Well, take a look at this picture of heart tissue that has been sitting in a ciborium in Lanciano, Italy since the 8th century and hasn't decayed without any preserving agents!"

Often times the response is a disinterested shrug, "Meh," or, "How do you know that story is even true? It's probably just a hoax." The real cause for their enduring skepticism and refusal to investigate further is an unwavering commitment to their worldview. The substantial Presence of Christ in the Eucharist simply won't fit in a box marked "materialism" or "naturalism." An atheist biologist, Richard Lewontin, wrote about this commitment that he and his fellow non-believing colleagues have:

> ...we have a prior commitment, a commitment to materialism...we are forced by our a priori [not based on experience] adherence to material causes to create an apparatus of investigation and a set of concepts that produce material explanations, no matter how counterintuitive, not matter how mystifying to the uninitiated. Moreover, that materialism is absolute, for we cannot allow a divine foot in the door.

In other words, "We need solid evidence before we will believe anything, but we're pretty sure we already know what reality should be like, so we've taken the liberty to define 'evidence' in such a way that we won't have to be bothered by any supernatural funny-business." Sounds pretty open-minded, right? At least he's honest, I suppose, because that's where you always have to begin in any search for the truth. If you find it hard to accept the Eucharist on scientific grounds, realize that the Church's claim about the Real Presence is not a scientific claim—it's a metaphysical (beyond physical) claim. It's ridiculous to think that the apostles only accepted what Jesus said because they were ignorant and believed that bread and wine changing into flesh and blood didn't violate the laws of nature. They accepted it because they believed the one making the claims to be the Son of God, the God who created the natural world and wrote its laws.

At the risk of taking up even more of your time, I'll conclude my thoughts here. If you're not Catholic, I hope you've learned a little more about what we believe regarding the Eucharist. If you are Catholic, I hope your understanding of the Eucharist has been illumined, your belief in it fortified, and your ability to articulate and defend that belief strengthened. I appreciate you taking time out of your day to read this longer-than-usual post, and I hope you enjoyed it! I'll leave you with this quote about the Eucharist from Saint Justin Martyr, who was one of the early Fathers of the Church, and a great defender of the Faith:

> We call this food Eucharist, and no one else is permitted to partake of it, except one who believes our teaching to be true and who has been washed in the washing that is for the remission of sins and for regeneration (i.e., has received baptism) and is thereby living as Chris enjoined. For not as common bread nor common drink do we receive these; but since Jesus Christ our Savior was made incarnate by the word of God and had both flesh and blood for our salvation, so too, as we have been taught, the food that has been made into the Eucharist by the eucharistic prayer set down by him, and by the change of which our blood and flesh is nurtured, is both the flesh and blood of that incarnated Jesus [First Apology 66 (c. A.D. 151)].

May God Bless you!

† Under the Mercy,

Chris Trummer

Sources:

Catholic Biblical Association (Great Britain). *The Holy Bible: Revised Standard Version, Catholic Edition*. New York: National Council of Churches of Christ in the USA, 1994. Print.

Catholic Church. *Lumen Gentium* in *Vatican II Documents*. Vatican City: Libreria Editrice Vaticana, 2011. Print.

Akin, James. *The Fathers Know Best*. Catholic Answers: San Diego, 2010. Print.

How to "Suck" at Your Critique of Religion

This post is a response to "How to Suck at Your Religion," an anti-religious comic strip from the website "The Oatmeal," created and ran by Matthew Inman. I read it recently after noticing a link to it on Facebook. After explaining a couple of my objections to the friend who posted it, I decided that it would be worthwhile to give the comic a more thorough treatment. This is not a rant or an emotional lashing out, but a calm and calculated response intended to set the record straight on some misinformation and misunderstandings. I will list all the questions posed in the comic and give a short response to each.

"Does your religion make you judge people?"

"Judge not, that you be not judged. For with the judgment you pronounce you will be judged, and the measure you give will be the measure you get" (Mt 7:1-2).
Since Jesus clearly taught us not to judge other people throughout the gospels, the answer is no, my religion does not "make me judge people"–it forbids me to do so. The fact that there are many hypocritical Christians who are judgmental, especially in modern countries like the U.S., is an unfortunate reality that tells us about those people, but not about Christianity itself. Saint Paul also warned the early Christians in Rome against judging others:

> Therefore you have no excuse, O man, whoever you are, when you judge another; for in passing judgment upon him you condemn yourself, because you, the judge, are doing the very same things (Rm 2:1).

"Does your religion hinder the advancement of science, technology, or medicine?"

Christianity provided the conceptual framework necessary for the use of scientific methodology, evidenced by the way science flourished in the Christian West as opposed to the non-Christian East, where the dominating philosophies typically saw physical reality as less predictable and intelligible. C.S. Lewis summarized this framework well in his book *Miracles*. He writes, "Men became scientific because they expected Law in Nature, and they expected Law in Nature because they believed in a Legislator" (Lewis). The Catholic Church founded the college system, the Laws of Evidence in science, and the first hospitals. Also, numerous Catholics throughout the centuries have been at the forefront of scientific progress. This is a list (but by no means an exhaustive one) of some of the most noteworthy Catholic men and women scientists:

Mariano Artigas (1938–2006) – Spanish physicist, philosopher and theologian who received the Templeton Foundation Prize in 1995.

André-Marie Ampère (1775–1836) – One of the main discoverers of electromagnetism

Stephen Barr (1953–present) – Professor in the Department of Physics and Astronomy at the University of Delaware and a member of its Bartol Research Institute

Henri Becquerel (1852–1908) – Awarded the Nobel Prize in physics for his co-discovery of radioactivity

Giovanni Alfonso Borelli (1608–1679) – Father of modern biomechanics

Louis Braille (1809–1852) – Inventor of the Braille reading and writing system

Gerty Cori (1896–1957) – Biochemist who was the first American woman win a Nobel Prize in science (1947)

Gaspard-Gustave Coriolis (1792–1843) – Formulated laws regarding rotating systems, which later became known as the Coriolis effect

Charles-Augustin de Coulomb (1736–1806) – Physicist who developed Coulomb's law

Nicolaus Copernicus (1473–1543) – Catholic cleric and first person to formulate a comprehensive heliocentric cosmology

René Descartes (1596–1650) – Father of modern philosophy and analytic geometry

Alberto Dou (1915-2009) – Spanish Jesuit priest who was president of the RoyalSociety of Mathematics, member of the Royal Academy of Natural, Physical, and Exact Sciences, and one of the foremost mathematicians of his country.

Enrico Fermi (1901–1954) – Awarded the Nobel Prize in physics for his work in induced radioactivity

Georges Lemaître (1894–1966) – Priest and Father of the Big Bang theory
Gregor Mendel (1822–1884) – Priest and Father of genetics
Johannes Peter Müller (1801–1858) – Founder of modern physiology
Blaise Pascal (1623–1662) – French mathematician, physicist, inventor, writer and philosopher
Anthony Rizzi (?–present) – Physicist who solved the problem of angular momentum in Einstein's Theory of General Relativity (1997), and founder and president of the Institute for Advanced Physics
Leonardo da Vinci (1452–1519) – Anatomist, scientist, mathematician, and painter
Alessandro Volta (1745–1827) – Physicist known for the invention of the battery

Given the large number of groundbreaking scientists who believed in the teachings of the Catholic Church and worked under her patronage, it's safe to say that the Church does not hinder the process of science, technology, or medicine. Here is the Church's view of science and its practice:

> Methodical research in all branches of knowledge, provided it is carried out in a truly scientific manner and does not override moral laws, can never conflict with the faith, because the things of the world and the things of faith derive from the same God. The humble and persevering investigator of the secrets of nature is being led, as it were, by the hand of God in spite of himself, for it is God, the conserver of all things, who made them what they are (Catechism of the Catholic Church 159).

Following this question, Inman digs up the dead horse of the Galileo controversy for beating. While there were certainly bishops and other people in the Church who opposed Galileo, their primary disagreement was on the grounds that he had not successfully proven his theory, which was true, since the observational technique he was using at the time, stellar parallax, could not definitively prove whether the Earth revolved around the Sun or vice-versa. Also, contrary to what the comic suggests, Galileo did not "spend the rest of his life in a dungeon." He was actually put on house arrest, and was treated quite well. This sentence was given to him because his work was being funded by the Church, and he disobeyed the pope's request that he wait until he had conclusive evidence to support his theory before claiming it to be fact. Galileo not only prematurely claimed his theory to be true, but openly mocked the pope with a cartoon character named *Simplicio*, which is Italian for "simple-minded" or "idiot." Non-Catholic historian of science, Gary Ferngren, concluded the following about how the Galileo affair has been historically understood:

> The traditional picture of Galileo as a martyr for intellectual freedom and as a victim of the Church's opposition to science has been demonstrated to be little more than a caricature (Ferngren).

"Did you choose your religion, or did someone else choose it for you?"

From the time I was a young child until my later teen years, I was Catholic more or less because my parents were Catholic. As we mature, we have to decide whether or not we really believe what we've been taught by our parents, whether we will claim the faith of our parents as our own or abandon it. To claim that a belief is false because of how that belief originated is known as the "genetic fallacy," a mistake commonly made by atheists when criticizing religious belief. The reason the genetic fallacy is so common is that it allows the person making it to think they have invalidated a person's beliefs, and so think they are justified in not listening to that person's actual reasons for believing. In addition to this point, there have been multitudes of highly educated people throughout history, as well as in modern times, who were not raised as Christians or even theists but came to believe later in life.

In this section of the comic, Inman also uses one of the most cliché and misunderstood images for God—an "invisible bearded flying man." This is such a mediocre oversimplification of what any serious monotheist means by the word "God" that it really doesn't even merit a response. However, there is at least one unintended but positive consequence of an atheist's use of images like this for God (and similar ones, e.g. the cosmic Santa Claus, sky fairy, flying spaghetti monster, etc.). The use of such images prevents the waste of precious time in argument, since the person who uses them immediately reveals that they know very little to nothing about theism or the classical arguments for the existence of God.

"Does your religion give you weird anxieties about your sexuality?"

The only anxieties I've had about my sexuality were present during my high school and early college years, when I had bought into the secular culture's idea of what the purpose of human sexuality is, namely, to provide pleasure and the immediate gratification of any and all sexual desires, regardless of whether or not they conform to the design or purpose inherent in the human body. The Church's teachings about human sexuality, especially as articulated by Saint John Paul II in his Theology of the Body, provide a clear, consistent, and complete understanding of the purpose and meaning of intimacy, marriage, and sexual unity between men and women. Without a basic understanding the Church's overall view of human nature, which is the foundation for her moral teaching as regards sexuality, it's difficult for non-believers to have productive dialogue with Catholics. It is no use to extract one specific teaching of the Church, say, the immorality of using contraception, and complain that it doesn't make any sense. To do this is to take out of context one piece that was meant to be understood as part of a whole, like examining a human kidney on a table and wondering, "What the heck is this thing for?" *Observe it inside of a body and you'll find out.*

"Do you validate your beliefs by constantly trying to convince other people to believe the same thing?"

> Jesus came and said to them, "All authority in heaven and on earth has been given to me. Go therefore and make disciples of all nations, baptizing them in the name of the Father and of the Son and of the Holy Spirit, teaching them to observe all that I have commanded you..." (Mt 28:18-20).

While it may not always be prudent or effective to go door-to-door like the followers of some religious traditions, as Inman pokes fun at, Jesus commanded (not suggested) that his disciples go forth and spread the Good News, the Gospel. Also, while it is uncharitable to "force your religion" on other people, it's a mistake to equate all efforts at evangelization to forcing or imposing. The role of the Church is to propose, not impose, Christ's message of Salvation to the world, and her mission is nothing other than the salvation of souls. This of course is only possible if Catholics are willing to take the time and effort to reach out to other people.

"Do you mock other religions for believing crazy things?"

I sincerely try not to mock other religions, although I have to admit that I am guilty of this at times. Again, far from being a feature of Christianity, the mockery of other religions by Christians constitutes a failure to love on their part. Also, it's hypocritical that Inman is condemning mockery here when he harshly mocks religion and religious people throughout this comic. The Catholic Church has a high respect for other religious traditions and their followers, as indicated in the following quote from the *Declaration on the Relation of the Church to Non-Christian Religions*:

> Other religions found everywhere try to counter the restlessness of the human heart, each in its own manner, by proposing "ways," comprising teachings, rules of life, and sacred rites. The Catholic Church rejects nothing that is true and holy in these religions. She regards with sincere reverence those ways of conduct and of life, those precepts and teachings which, though differing in many aspects from the ones she holds and sets forth, nonetheless often reflect a ray of that Truth which enlightens all men. Indeed, she proclaims, and ever must proclaim Christ 'the way, the truth, and the life' (John 14:6), in whom men may find the fullness of religious life, in whom God has reconciled all things to Himself (*Nostra Aetate* 2).

"Do you vote based solely on your religious beliefs?"

Given how foundational religious beliefs are to a person's understanding of reality, is it really any surprise to the skeptic that religious people would vote primarily on the basis of those beliefs? A person's religious beliefs include their understanding of what human beings are, what our purpose is, what constitutes authentic human flourishing, and what our natural rights are based on these factors. That being said, what ideas could be more fundamental that a religious person should vote based on those instead? I can think of none. For example, if my beliefs tell me that all human beings have the right to life, even unborn children, then I can only conclude that abortion is a gross violation of basic human rights and dignity. Therefore, while there are certainly other important issues in need of consideration, none of them can take political precedence over an issue as paramount as abortion.

"Are you so dangerously extremist that even a silly web cartoonist can't draw a picture of your prophet without fearing for his life?"

This is clearly a shot at Islam, and at Islamic extremists in particular, so I don't feel that it's necessary for me to offer a response on behalf of Christianity. In fact, this is one of the few questions that I actually found to be a fair one, and any Muslim who is that extreme and violent should certainly reexamine himself or herself, because such conduct is by no means a necessary or even mainstream interpretation of the Quran.

"Would you die for your religion?"

> Martyrdom is the supreme witness given to the truth of the faith: it means bearing witness even unto death. The martyr bears witness to Christ who died and rose, to whom he is united by charity. He bears witness to the truth of the faith and of Christian doctrine. He endures death through an act of fortitude (*Catechism of the Catholic Church* 2473).

If by, "Would you die for your religion?" the question intends to ask, "Would you die before renouncing your religious beliefs?" then I would like to think that, if faced with either rejecting my faith in Christ and living, or remaining faithful to Him and dying, I would choose the latter and be counted among the countless martyrs who have witnessed to Christianity over the last 2000 years. However, since I can't begin to imagine being in such a terrifying situation, I can't say definitively that I would die for my religion—I might be too much of a coward. Dying for what you believe is by no means unique to Christianity, and a willingness to die for your beliefs does not in itself prove that your beliefs are true. However, it does prove that you are sincere in your belief (liars make terrible martyrs) and so the person who objects to your beliefs must do so on grounds of reason and historical evidence, instead of attacking your motives for believing.

"Would you kill for your religion? [Or] hurt, hinder, or condemn in the name of God?"

> "You have heard that it was said to the men of old, 'You shall not kill; and whoever kills shall be liable to judgment.' But I say to you that every one who is angry with his brother shall be liable to judgment; whoever insults his brother shall be liable to the council, and whoever says, 'You fool!' shall be liable to the hell of fire" (Mt 5:21-22).

It is necessary here to distinguish between killing as a means of conquest, terror, or oppression, versus killing as a means of self-defense or defense of innocent life. The former is clearly inconsistent with the teachings of Christ, while the latter can be justifiable, according to Catholic moral teaching, provided certain conditions are met. These conditions are outlined in the *Catechism of the Catholic Church*, and they include:

> The damage inflicted by the aggressor on the nation or community of nations must be lasting, grave, and certain; All other means of putting an end to it must have been shown to be impractical or ineffective; There must be serious prospects of success; The use of arms must not produce evils and disorders graver than the evil to be eliminated. The power of modern means of destruction weighs very heavily in evaluating this condition (2309).

To answer the question then, if I perceived a threat to my life or the lives of other innocent people, and the above conditions were met (as well as I could determine given the amount of time I had to respond), then yes, I would take another person's life. It is because of this understanding that I have no reservations about being a member of the Illinois National Guard, in an infantry unit that has deployed for combat operations to both Iraq and Afghanistan (before I was there).

"Does your religion inspire you to help people?"

> "If any one has the world's goods and sees his brother in need, yet closes his heart against him, how does God's love abide in him? Little children, let us not love in word or speech but in deed and in truth" (1 Jn 3:17-18).

> Let each of you look not only to his own interests, but also to the interests of others (Php 2:4).

> "Truly, I say to you, as you did it to one of the least of these my brethren, you did it to me" (Mt 25:40).

It's ironic (but not surprising) how this question presupposes that helping people is good and something that we should all do. When Christians fail to help others whom they are fully capable of helping, they are failing to love as their Savior commanded them, and therefore living in a manner that is inconsistent with their worldview. On the other hand, atheists who fail to help others whom they are fully capable of helping are living in a manner *consistent* with their worldview, since their view maintains that human beings are randomly evolved collections of matter with no real purpose or destination. Regardless of what a person believes about God, everyone believes that you should always obey your own conscience. This uniquely human faculty puts us in touch with objective moral values and duties that are real and binding, regardless of time, place, or culture. This is why, despite the efforts people make to avail themselves of it, they find the moral law inescapable. Saint Paul had this insight:

> When Gentiles who have not the law do by nature what the law requires, they are a law to themselves, even though they do not have the law. They show that what the law requires is written on their hearts, while their conscience also bears witness and their conflicting thoughts accuse or perhaps excuse them on that day when, according to my gospel, God judges the secrets of men by Christ Jesus (Rm 2:14-16).

"Does it make you happier?"

Having spent several years chasing happiness using all of the world's methods, including popularity, money, possessions, drinking, partying, shallow relationships, with a pervading sense of selfishness throughout, I can say with confidence that my religion makes me happier. The happiness does not come from delusion, like the popular delusion of spending all of your time worrying about your looks, your car, the number of "likes" on your Facebook post, or your favorite sports team, none of which offer any real or lasting meaning. Rather, the happiness that my faith gives me is in the hope that comes from placing my trust in God, admitting to Him my brokenness, experiencing His love and forgiveness, and striving to love him more each day. As Saint Faustina wrote in her diary:

> I want to love You as no human soul has ever loved You before; and although I am utterly miserable and small, I have nevertheless cast the anchor of my trust deep down into the abyss of Your mercy (*Divine Mercy in My Soul* 283).

"Does it help you cope with the fact that you are a bag of meat sitting on a rock in outer space, and that someday you will DIE, and you are completely powerless, helpless, and insignificant in the wake of this beautiful cosmic [crap]storm we call existence? If it helps you with that, carry on with your religion – just keep it to yourself."

This is a textbook example of *begging the question*, which is a type of circular reasoning in which the conclusion is assumed to be true. The person asking the question hasn't established the truth of part of their question or argument. An example of this would be the question, "Have you stopped beating your wife?" One of the funny things about this comic is that, with all of the questions it asks about "your religion," it never bothers to ask about the truth of any religion. *Is it true?* The only reason anyone in the world should ever believe anything at all is *because it's true*, not because it suits your personality, makes you feel better, or because it is useful to yourself or to society. The comment at the end, "If it helps you with that, carry on with your religion," is not a gesture of good will but a patronizing insult, a pat on the head as if to say "Aww, isn't he just adorable with his cute little religious beliefs!"

The Problem With Skepticism

Instead of an honest search for the truth and an openness to the possibility that what some religion teaches might actually be true, or at least have some elements of truth in it, skeptics like the author of this comic presume from the outset of discussion that all religion is unreasonable and ridiculous. Typically, such people maintain that they will only believe something if it can be shown to be true by the scientific method. This view, known as "scientism," is self-destructive, since it is itself not a scientific claim but a philosophical one, and therefore not provable by the scientific method. This philosophy is a convenient one to hold, and is often the mark of an intellectually lazy or prideful person. Instead of promoting a fruitful dialogue, the skeptic merely affords himself the luxury of sitting back and criticizing the beliefs of everyone else, spending all of his time on the offense, since he has no positive content of his own to defend. When your world view exists only as a negation or rejection of another world view, you're inevitably going to find yourself becoming increasingly close-minded, negative, and incapable of relating well to others.

      Mr. Inman did well to add the words "someday you will DIE" in this last question. Indeed, some day we will all die. I can only hope and pray that he, along with his audience members who criticize and mock religion and religious people with such pride and confidence, approach their own deaths with much greater humility and openness—it could make an eternal difference for them. This comic is nothing more than a collection of myths, clichés, and misunderstandings. However, it may be useful for at least one thing—as an exercise for students in an Intro to Logic class to help them recognize logical fallacies. Hopefully, through continued efforts in education, especially in the areas of history and philosophy, websites such as The Oatmeal will eventually have no audience through which to spread such gross distortions about religion and religious people. That is one of the downsides of the internet, namely, that it makes it possible for people with little to no credibility on a subject to spread misinformation about it like a cancer. Fortunately, even a cancer can be treated and put into remission.

Thank you for reading, and God bless!

† Under the Mercy,

Chris Trummer

Sources:

Catholic Biblical Association (Great Britain). *The Holy Bible: Revised Standard Version, Catholic Edition*. New York: National Council of Churches of Christ in the USA, 1994. Print.

Catholic Church. *Catechism of the Catholic Church*. 2nd Ed. Washington, DC: United States Catholic Conference, 2000. Print.

Catholic Church. *Nostra Aetate. Vatican II Documents*. Vatican City: Libreria Editrice Vaticana, 2011. Print.

C.S. Lewis. *Miracles*. London & Glasgow: Collins/Fontana, 1947. 2002 Edition. Print.

Ferngren, Gary, ed. *Science and Religion: A Historical Introduction*. JHU Press, 2002. Print.

Kowalska, Maria Faustina. *Divine Mercy In My Soul*. Marian Press, 2003. Print.

Four Views on Suffering

The existence of suffering, or "problem" of suffering as it's known in philosophy, is a puzzling and unavoidable fact of reality. Nobody questions that we suffer, the question is, "Why do we suffer?" This question has weighed heavily on the minds of human beings since the dawn of our existence. The answer to this question is found in how we view reality, more specifically, in how we view human beings. This isn't to say that the answer is only relative to our personal beliefs, but that if suffering does have meaning, then its meaning must be bound up with the rest of reality. To help us understand suffering more clearly, let's use Jesus' parable about Lazarus and the rich man as a model, and consider how four different world views would understand the story. The question we need to keep in mind while examining these four different worldviews is: What is a human being?

There was a rich man, who was clothed in purple and fine linen and who feasted sumptuously every day. And at his gate lay a poor man named Lazarus, full of sores, who desired to be fed with what fell from the rich man's table; moreover the dogs came and licked his sores. The poor man died and was carried by the angels to Abraham's bosom. The rich man also died and was buried; and in Hades, being in torment, he lifted up his eyes, and saw Abraham far off and Lazarus in his bosom. And he called out, 'Father Abraham, have mercy upon me, and send Lazarus to dip the end of his finger in water and cool my tongue; for I am in anguish in this flame.' But Abraham said, 'Son, remember that you in your lifetime received your good things, and Lazarus in like manner evil things; but now he is comforted here, and you are in anguish. And besides all this, between us and you a great chasm has been fixed, in order that those who would pass from here to you may not be able, and none may cross from there to us.' And he said, 'Then I beg you, father, to send him to my father's house, for I have five brothers, so that he may warn them, lest they also come into this place of torment.' But Abraham said, 'They have Moses and the prophets; let them hear them.' And he said, 'No, father Abraham; but if some one goes to them from the dead, they will repent.' He said to him, 'If they do not hear Moses and the prophets, neither will they be convinced if some one should rise from the dead' (Lk 16:19-31).

Buddhism

Let's begin with Buddhism. Siddhartha Gautama (who is considered the original Buddha) founded an entire philosophy-religion (neither term describes Buddhism exactly) on the idea of suffering (*dukkha*), so surely he can provide us with some insights. Buddha believed that all suffering is the result of ignorance and attachment. This ignorance is of the fact that there is no human "self," and this attachment is a craving for the permanence of the self and the material world. Buddha then discerned a way by which one could eliminate all suffering – by eliminating all desire. In an effort to eliminate the effect, suffering, he had to eliminate the cause, desire. That's an awfully high price to pay, considering how deeply our desires are engrained into our human nature. Buddha believed that ignorance resulted from "grasping at what you can't have" and "avoiding what you cannot avoid," and yet the whole purpose of the Noble Eightfold Path of Buddhism is an attempt to grasp at what one cannot have, namely, a life free of all suffering, and to avoid what one cannot avoid—suffering—even if achieving this means viewing all of physical reality as an illusion. When trying to understand reality, we naturally seek to have a clear picture of everything, to come up with an explanation that takes into account all of the data. The problem with Buddhism then is that it does not account for all of the data. A good Buddhist would try to relieve Lazarus' suffering by helping him realize that his body is an illusion. This seems to be an extreme case of "throwing the baby out with the bathwater." Most people, especially those educated in Western countries, simply can't accept the idea that the world around them, which they experience constantly and directly through their senses, is an illusion. It is no coincidence that the physical sciences failed to take root for so long in Eastern countries; the total skepticism towards any knowledge derived from observation, which consists of sensory data, is directly opposed to the scientific method (for more on this topic, see my post, "How to Suck at Your Critique of Religion").

Hinduism

Next, let's consider how a Hindu would see Lazarus in the parable. Lazarus would be considered one of the Dalits, or "outcastes." In the traditional Hindu caste system, people are understood to suffer more or less based on which caste they're in, which is determined by the amount of "karma" they have accumulated in their past lives. In order to achieve *moksha* (liberation) from the Samsara (reincarnation) cycle, a person must "burn off" all of their karma through *dukkha* (suffering), which might take literally thousands of lifetimes. With this understanding, any attempt to relieve the suffering of another person would be seen as an interference, since doing so would only prevent them from burning off their karma, and so ultimately prolong their suffering. The Dalits are so low in the Hindu view of human beings that they are not even part of a caste, hence the term,"out-castes." For centuries, approximately 25% of the Indian population were considered to be Dalits, until about 60 years ago when the Indian government abolished the caste system. Unfortunately, there is evidence that the caste mindset is still very much present in India today. From the standpoint of history, we know that every widespread violation of basic human dignity and rights has been made possible by the redefining of a group, class, or race of people as "subhuman" or even "non-human." The fact that this redefinition is even necessary testifies to the universal truth of morality that is written on the heart of every person. Knowing this, along with our human tendency to justify our behavior whenever possible, it's easy to see how the Hindu caste mentality can be a tempting ideology (if suffering is what liberates people, then I'm not obligated to help relieve their suffering). However, if the way we view human beings clashes with our natural inclinations to ensure justice and relieve suffering, then we should reevaluate our world view – not disregard our inclinations. The best Hindu advice on how to treat Lazarus would be, "Ignore him, he needs to burn off his karma." Somehow, this just sounds like a cop out, because instead of motivating us to help the suffering people who we encounter, it simply lets us off the hook and enables us to be selfish. The Hindu solution to the problem of suffering is a very human one.

Atheism

Now, let's have a word for our non-believing friends, the atheists. First, let's answer our guiding question, "What is a human being?" from an atheist standpoint. Who better to speak for atheism than Bertrand Russell? Russell was a British mathematician, logician, philosopher, author, and one of the most influential atheists of the twentieth century. He wrote the following about what a human being is:

> Man is the product of causes which had no prevision of the end they were achieving; that his origin, his growth, his hopes and fears, his loves and his beliefs, are but the outcome of accidental collocations of atoms; that no fire, no heroism, no intensity of thought and feeling, can preserve an individual life beyond the grave; that all the labors of the ages, all the devotion, all the inspiration, all the noonday brightness of human genius, are destined to extinction in the vast death of the solar system, and that the whole temple of Man's achievement must inevitably be buried beneath the débris of a universe in ruins—all these things, if not quite beyond dispute, are yet so nearly certain, that no philosophy which rejects them can hope to stand. Only within the scaffolding of these truths, only on the firm foundation of unyielding despair, can the soul's habitation henceforth be safely built (*Free Man's Worship*).

No philosophy which rejects them can hope to stand. Since the dawn of the twentieth century when Russell wrote this, the number of people who attend church services regularly in modern countries has indeed decreased, along with the number of people who identify with a particular religious tradition or denomination. However, Russell probably would have been shocked (and disappointed) if he were still alive today, because the number of people who claim to be atheists has barely increased in modern countries, and hasn't increased at all on a global scale. Theistic philosophies still dominate the world, and they don't appear to be going anywhere anytime soon. However, the question still remains to be answered – was Russell right? Are we nothing more than collections of matter resulting from blind and random purely physical processes? Without getting into a lengthy philosophical discussion about materialism

66

and naturalism, let's limit ourselves for the time being to the implications of holding such a world view.

An atheist cannot describe suffering as being objectively "worse" than happiness, because in his view,"suffering" and "happiness" are just labels that human beings created to describe reality. In the case of happiness, this set of neurons is firing in the brain, in the case of suffering, a different set of neurons is firing. Once you begin to describe one scenario as "better" than the other, you have stepped into the realm of value and meaning, which cannot be real and objective in a purely material universe. Atoms are not good or evil, true or false, so neither is a collection of them, however intricate and complicated their arrangement may be. If atheism is true, then Lazarus, while we might label him as a "human being" who has "dignity" and the "right to life," is really nothing more than a collection of matter, a group of chemical reactions that happen to be existing together in the same location. Therefore, for a consistent atheist, the most humane thing to do with Lazarus would be to either ignore him or to put him out of his misery, since he otherwise might become a burden to other "collections of matter." We do this with our pets all the time, and it's usually considered loving and merciful – why not with human beings? What makes killing them so wrong? Fyodor Dostoyevsky famously summarized this in his epic novel, *The Brothers Karamazov*, writing "If God does not exist, all things are permissible".

If reading this makes you recoil, that's good—that means that you haven't lost your sense of humanity. The reason that our conscience has the authority to command us to sympathize with, assist, and love our fellow human beings, even when doing so does not provide us with any perceivable advantage in terms of survival, is because our conscience is not simply a biological faculty. The realm of morality is so evident and immediately experienced by us that only very intelligent people are usually clever enough to fool themselves into believing it doesn't exist. By asserting that human beings are nothing more than matter, the atheist inadvertently denies the existence of human personhood. If suffering, along with all human efforts to explain and understand it, is nothing more than a material phenomenon, then the answer to the question of why we suffer is, "There is no answer, suffering is as meaningless as the rest of reality."

Christianity

Now that we've examined the problem of suffering from the standpoint of three other world views, let's answer the question, "How would a Christian see Lazarus?" One of the luxuries of the Christian world view is that, when determining how a Christian should see something, one need only answer, "How would Christ see this?" Jesus Christ did not claim simply to know a way to happiness, or the truth, or what constitutes authentic human living. He claimed to be "the way, the truth, and the life" (Jn 14:6). If Jesus is the truth, what is his answer to the problem of suffering? His answer comes not in word, but in action:

> Christ Jesus...though he was in the form of God, did not count equality with God a thing to be grasped, but emptied himself, taking the form of a servant, being born in the likeness of men. And being found in human form he humbled himself and became obedient unto death, even death on a cross (Php 2:5-7).

When Jesus' friend Lazarus (not the same guy from the above parable) died, even though Jesus had the power to raise him from the dead, and even though he must have ultimately known the meaning and value of suffering, his reaction was described in just two words: "Jesus wept" (Jn 11:35). Those two words tell us a tremendous amount about what God thinks about human suffering. It is difficult. Being optimistic, knowing the temporary nature of the suffering, and even knowing its cause does not make enduring it easy. This is why even Christ prayed that he wouldn't have to suffer his passion and death: "Father, if thou art willing, remove this cup from me; nevertheless not my will, but thine, be done" (Lk 22:42). One of the unfortunate effects of limiting your view of reality to only material or natural explanations is that it closes your mind off to one of the most powerful and uniquely human capacities, the ability to recognize symbols. A symbol is something that points beyond itself, that has its meaning outside of itself. You can see a simple yet profound and beautiful example of this right now as you read this sentence—language. Like the words of a love poem, a captivating novel, or the lyrics of a beautiful hymn, everything in the physical world, suffering included, points to something beyond itself. All of reality is like a story, and that suffering, an ever present and undeniable part of that reality, should have meaning simply fits the narrative better. Other worldviews try to downplay or even deny suffering; Christianity transforms it. Christ did not come to rescue us from the suffering of this life, as if suffering were something to be avoided at all costs, but to plunge us deeper into the mystery of it, since entering fully into that mystery is the key to unlocking the meaning of life. If God exists, and he is all-knowing, all-good, and all-powerful, then the reason we suffer must be because we need to. However, God does not leave us to fend for ourselves, even in this life. By the Incarnation of God in the person of Jesus Christ, and by his death and resurrection, we can have the sure hope that our suffering has meaning, and that God is capable of bringing good out of even the worst sufferings in our lives. Saint Paul, who suffered terrible persecution and was eventually beheaded for his faith in Christ, wrote the following about what suffering means in the context of the Christian faith: "I consider that the sufferings of this present time are not worth comparing with the glory that is to be revealed to us" (Rm 8:18).

Not worth comparing. How could Saint Paul say that? Did he live a sheltered life or something? Was he delusional? No. He could say it because he had come into contact with infinite love, with Love itself – Jesus Christ. In the face of infinite love, finite suffering is literally "not worth comparing." At the end of his novel *The Bridge of San Luis Rey*, Thornton Wilder spelled out the two possible explanations of the problem of suffering in the following way:

> Some say that we shall never know, and that to the gods we are like flies that boys kill on a summer day, and others say that the very sparrows do not lose a feather that has not been brushed away by the finger of God.

Both cannot be true. How do we live our lives? Do we trust that God is ultimately in control and that Saint Paul was correct in saying that "in everything God works for good with those who love him, who are called according to his purpose?" (Rm 8:28). Let's ask God to give us the grace to trust him with everything, even with the suffering in our life, which too often confuses us and makes us doubt his infinite love for us.

† Under the Mercy,

Chris Trummer

Sources:

Catholic Biblical Association (Great Britain). *The Holy Bible: Revised Standard Version, Catholic Edition*. New York: National Council of Churches of Christ in the USA, 1994. Print.

Russell, Bertrand. *Free Man's Worship*. 1903.

Wilder, Thornton. *The Bridge of San Luis Rey*. 1927.

What Christmas Means to Me

In the midst of the annual chaos that has become a trademark of this time of year, it's important for each of us to ask ourselves, "What does Christmas really mean to me?" Is it just a time for delicious food, sweet deals at all of the stores, and the chance to get my hands on the latest gadget or other gift that I'm hoping to receive? The "real meaning of Christmas" has been at the forefront of my mind, so I'd like to share my thoughts here.

First and foremost, I see Christmas as a celebration of the turning point in God's great narrative of Creation. The birth of Jesus Christ in history marks the beginning of the climax in "the greatest story ever told." God's story has the most epic plot twist, but unlike other plot twists, which involve unexpected encounters between the characters in the story, this twist involves an unexpected encounter between the characters and the author. Peter Kreeft pointed out this idea in his talk titled "Shocking Beauty," when he made an analogy between the story of Creation and *The Lord of the Rings*: "Imagine Frodo Baggins meeting, not Gandalf, not Aragorn, but *Tolkien*; Macbeth meeting, not King Duncan, not Macduff, but *Shakespeare*." This is exactly what did happen almost two thousand years ago, when God, the divine author of all Creation, seeing that we were helpless against our enemy, sin, cast Himself into his own story as the human character of Jesus Christ. This is what separates Christianity from every other religion, namely, that the truth of it rests entirely on historical claims. If the Jewish prophets never actually foretold a coming Messiah, then no one would have recognized Jesus as someone special, since moral teachers and all types of gurus were extremely common during that time. If Jesus never actually taught his apostles everything contained in the Gospels, then there would be no Christianity. If the Resurrection never actually happened, then thousands of early Christians wouldn't have been willing to endure persecution, torture, and death at the hands of their Roman oppressors. Obviously, all of these historical claims depend on the fact that Jesus really existed, that he was actually born into the world at a point in history.

While all of this is crucially important, knowing that Jesus existed is not what Christmas itself is all about, and certainly not what Christmas means to me. I would argue that, rather than being primarily about the fact that God entered into his Creation, Christmas is more about celebrating the way in which God chose to enter Creation. While the theological concept of the Incarnation may seem somewhat abstract and difficult to understand, the birth of a tiny baby boy to a teenage girl in a little town in Israel is simple, concrete, and beautiful. That is why the same simple hymns bring joy to our hearts and tears to our eyes year after year. "Fall on your knees! O hear the angel voices!"

Christmas is the annual retelling of the greatest story ever told: We are lost sheep, and the Shepard has come. Let's pray that we may all experience the birth of Jesus as a concrete event, one that changes our hearts and the way we view the world. In the words of Pope Emeritus Benedict XVI, "The one who has hope lives differently." Hope is exactly what we have when we live the reality of Christmas. Emmanuel! God is with us!

† Under the Mercy,

Chris Trummer

Salvation Outside of the Church

"Extra Ecclesiam nulla salus."

This Latin phrase translates to, "Outside of the Church there is no salvation." Its original use comes from Saint Cyprian of Carthage, who was a 3rd century bishop and one of the Fathers of the Church. Does it sound harsh? Extreme? Archaic? Exclusive? Judgmental? All of the above? You may be surprised or even (but hopefully not) scandalized to hear that the Catholic Church maintains the truth of this statement to this day. The problem is, most non-Catholics today, and unfortunately many Catholics, don't understand what is meant by the word "Church." When most people hear the word "Church," they are probably thinking of: 1) the building where people gather to worship, 2) the hierarchical or institutional structure of the Church, or 3) the collective group of people who make up the Church, the Body of Christ. The correct definition of the Church is: all of the above—and more. In *Lumen Gentium*, the Second Vatican Council said the following of the Church:

> Basing itself on Scripture and Tradition, the Council teaches that the Church, a pilgrim now on earth, is necessary for salvation: the one Christ is the mediator and the way of salvation; he is present to us in his body which is the Church. He himself explicitly asserted the necessity of faith and Baptism, and thereby affirmed at the same time the necessity of the Church which men enter through Baptism as through a door. Hence they could not be saved who, knowing that the Catholic Church was founded as necessary by God through Christ, would refuse either to enter it or to remain in it (LG 14).

Salvation Comes Through Christ Alone

Jesus Christ said, "I am the way, and the truth, and the life; no man comes to the Father, but by me"(Jn 14:6). Saint Peter later testified to this truth of Christ being the only source of salvation: "And there is salvation in no one else, for there is no other name under heaven given among men by which we must be saved"(Acts 4:12). Rightly then, the Catholic Church has always upheld and taught the truth that salvation for each individual person is only possible because of the merits of Jesus Christ, namely, because of his Passion, Death, and Resurrection. That being said, what are we to make of the billions of people who have lived and died without having any explicit belief in or even knowledge of the person of Jesus Christ? Are they simply "out of luck" as it were? Did God will that some people would be born in non-Christian or even anti-Christian environments, and expect them to, against all odds and in spite of all psychological, social, and cultural obstacles, come to believe in Jesus Christ and be received into the Catholic Church? What happens to Jews, Muslims, Hindus, Buddhists, and all other non-Christian or even non-religious people when they die? Given the fact that Christians only comprise approximately one-third of the world's population, these questions are extremely relevant, unless we are content to write off two-thirds of humanity to damnation. It is important that we try to understand God's plan of salvation for humanity and the Church's role in bringing that plan to fruition.

God Wills That All Be Saved

First, let's review our data about God's plan for humanity. In Saint Paul's first letter to Timothy, he writes that God "...wills that all men be saved and come to a knowledge of the truth"(2:4). What is Saint Paul saying here? Is he endorsing "universal salvation," the theory that everyone will eventually be saved and that there effectively is no hell or eternal damnation? Absolutely not! When God created human beings with free will, He necessarily gave up the possibility that His will would always be done, which is why we pray during the Our Father, "Thy will be done on earth as it is in Heaven" - if it were already being done, there would be no need to pray for it! What Saint Paul is saying here is that God has made it possible for every person to be saved. If God wills the salvation of everyone, and He is omnipotent (all-powerful) and omniscient (all-knowing), then salvation must be at least possible for everyone. In other words, if someone isn't saved, it can only be their fault, not God's. So, where does Jesus fit into all of this? Well, if a person did not know Jesus during their lifetime, because they never heard the Gospel or at least never heard it presented in an intelligible way, then when they die, while they might not be saved, they will not be condemned on the basis of their lack of belief in Jesus Christ.

Objective Fact vs. Subjective Knowledge

This brings up an essential distinction about salvation and Christ. The distinction is between the objective fact that Jesus Christ is the only possible source of salvation and the subjective knowledge that each individual must possess in order to secure that salvation. The Catholic Church teaches that it is possible for persons who have no subjective knowledge of Christ to be saved:

> Those who, through no fault of their own, do not know the Gospel of Christ or his Church, but who nevertheless seek God with a sincere heart, and, moved by grace, try in their actions to do his will as they know it through the dictates of their conscience—those too may achieve eternal salvation (LG 16).

Let's be clear, acknowledging the possibility of salvation for non-Christians does not change the fact that, if such persons are saved, they are saved only by the merits of Jesus Christ. For example, if a Hindu is saved, he or she is not saved by Hinduism, but by Christ. If a Muslim dies and is received by God into Heaven, he or she is not "bypassing" the need for Christ as a savior, they simply must have accepted Christ implicitly by the way they lived their life, seeking to do God's will and admitting their need for forgiveness. Some people reject this idea entirely, and instead argue that a person cannot be saved unless they explicitly profess belief in Jesus Christ, (and in some traditions, pray the "Sinner's Prayer"). The problem with this idea is multi-faceted. First, there is the problem of the retroactive application of the salvific grace of Christ's sacrifice. In other words, what about the people who lived before the time of Christ, such as Abraham, Moses, Elijah, the prophets, and the rest of God's chosen people? Obviously, none of them believed in Jesus in any explicit way, because he wasn't even born yet! But wait, didn't Moses and Elijah appear with Jesus during his Transfiguration on Mount Tabor? Yes, they did, and so apparently they had been saved. Clearly then, there must be more to salvation than just believing in Jesus and reciting the Sinner's Prayer.

If Knowledge, How Much?

There is another problem with the idea that subjective knowledge of Christ is necessary for salvation. If a person must have personal knowledge of Christ in order to be saved, the question immediately arises, "How much knowledge?" Do you simply need to believe that Jesus was a great moral teacher or guru and try to imitate him, or do you have to believe that he was Divine and the Son of God? Can you believe that Jesus was half God and half man, or do you have to believe that he was fully God and fully man? Do you have to believe in his literal, bodily Resurrection, or can you believe that he "spiritually rose" in the hearts of his disciples? Can you believe that the Eucharist is only a symbol of Jesus' body and blood, or do you have to believe the Catholic doctrine that the Eucharist substantially becomes Jesus' body, blood, soul, and divinity? In other words, where do you draw the line? If a certain amount of knowledge is necessary for salvation, that would imply that when you die, God effectively gives you a theology exam; if you pass, you go to heaven; if you fail, you go to hell. Somehow, this just doesn't seem right! Is God judging our souls or only our minds? Is a self-righteous and heartless rich man who believes in Jesus and goes to Mass on Sundays closer to being saved than a homeless and desperate addict, who steals food to survive because he doesn't know what else to do, but is trying to seek help? As usual, our friend Saint Paul is here to help us answer these difficult questions. In his letter to the Romans, he explains the expectations of those who do not believe in Jesus or know about his teaching:

> When Gentiles who have not the law do by nature what the law requires, they are a law to themselves, even though they do not have the law. They show that what the law requires is written on their hearts, while their conscience also bears witness and their conflicting thoughts accuse or perhaps excuse them on that day when, according to my gospel, God judges the secrets of men by Christ Jesus (Rm 2:14-17).

What the law requires is written on their hearts. This means that they can know what is essential to living a moral life by their own conscience and human reasoning. He then says that the conflicting thoughts of men who do not believe in Christ can "accuse or perhaps excuse them" when they are judged by Christ. This means that those who did not know Christ during their earthly lives will not be surprised or dissatisfied with the way they are judged, because their own conscience has already condemned them, and they unfortunately refused to listen.

The Two Natures of Christ

There is one last element that is crucial to understanding God's plan of salvation for mankind, and that is the nature of Jesus Christ. Who is Jesus Christ? Was he the 33-year-old Jewish carpenter who was condemned to death for blasphemy and executed almost 2000 years ago? Yes, but he is so much more than that! Jesus Christ is fully human, but also fully divine. He is the Son of God and the Second Person of the Holy Trinity. While he became incarnate as a human infant at a specific time in history, he always was, is now, and always will be, God. He was not only a historical figure, but the Eternal Word of the Father, by whom and through whom everything that exists was created. Saint John explains this beautifully in the prologue of his gospel:

> In the beginning was the Word, and the Word was with God, and the Word was God. He was in the beginning with God; all things were made through him, and without him was not anything made that was made (Jn 1:1-3).

What does all of this mean? A lot, actually. If Jesus is the source of everything that exists, then it makes sense that there would be numerous ways of knowing him. In other words, a person can know Christ in ways besides knowing him as the 33 year-old Jewish carpenter, even if that is an important part of the complete truth about who Jesus is. Saint John implies that Christ can be known in some way by all people, regardless of their education, culture, and when or where they lived: "In [Christ] was life, and the life was the light of men...The true light that enlightens every man was coming into the world (Jn 1:4,9).

The Logos and the Tao

Saint John wrote that Christ is the light that enlightens all men, not just a select lucky few who happened to live in the towns where he preached, taught, and worked miracles. How can this be true? It's true because Christ is the Eternal Logos (Word), and therefore is not bound by the space, time, and material limitations that he willingly embraced during his time on earth. In many Asian countries, there is a belief in the "Tao" (pronounced "dow"), which is the "way" or "path" that creates and orders everything in the universe. The Tao is considered to be the source of everything in reality, and those who follow the Tao strive to live in a way that conforms to it's way or pattern. Such conformity consists of doing things in accordance with their nature, which creates "effortless action." Living by the Tao is supposed to bring the person peace and render morality, in the sense of rules, laws, and government, obsolete. There is an interesting parallel between the Taoist concept of the Tao and the Christian concept of the Logos. In Saint John's gospel, when he writes that Christ is the "Word," the Greek word that he actually used was "Logos." Logos can be translated many ways, including: word, thought, speech, way, and path. When Christianity spread to China, and the Chinese people came to understand who Jesus Christ was, they translated "Logos" as "Tao" (e.g., "And the Tao became flesh, and dwelt among us.") This marriage of Asian philosophy and religion with the very heart of Christianity is very significant, and beautifully so, because it reveals a universality in our human search for God (or rather, in God's search for us). If we are made from love, by love, and for love, then how could any honest person's search for the truth lead him to anything other than Love himself in the flesh, Jesus Christ? Later in John's gospel, Jesus speaks about how he wants to reach out to all people, even those normally excluded by the Jewish mindset:

I am the good shepherd; I know my own and my own know me, as the Father knows me and I know the Father; and I lay down my life for the sheep. And I have other sheep, that are not of this fold; I must bring them also, and they will heed my voice. So there shall be one flock, one shepherd (Jn 10:14-16).

Don't Limit God!

As we can see, God's plans are bigger and better than ours! We tend to limit God, to put Him in a box made of our preconceptions and narrow-mindedness. If a sentence starts with: "God wouldn't...", "God can't...", or "God doesn't care about..." then it's probably wrong. Much of our spiritual growth is the continual process of shedding off our old ideas about God, adopting new ones, finding them insufficient, shedding those off...and repeating the cycle. This should come as no surprise, since we are finite beings and God is infinite, we can never have a complete understanding of Him. This includes God's means of bringing about salvation, and how His universal love for all of mankind is made manifest in our world of spatial, temporal, and material limitations. Hopefully, through prayer, study, and life experience, we can eventually learn to "let God be God," and instead of asking with the apostles, "Lord, will those who are saved be few?"(Lk 13:23) we will instead get out into the vineyard, where "the harvest is plentiful, but the laborers are few"(Mt 9:37).

The Church is All-Inclusive

When we say that there is no salvation outside of the Catholic Church, we must realize that this is not an exclusive statement that condemns the lost sheep or those who are "of another flock," but rather, an inclusive statement, one that signifies just how universal the reach, responsibility, and mission of the Catholic Church is in the world. There is no need for us to fully understand how and if a particular non-Christian will be saved before we can witness the truth of Christianity to him or her, so what are we waiting for? Jesus gave us no reason to delay!

Go therefore and make disciples of all nations, baptizing them in the name of the Father and of the Son and of the Holy Spirit, teaching them to observe all that I have commanded you; and behold, I am with you always, to the close of the age (Mt 28:19-20).

† Under the Mercy,

Chris Trummer

What Serving Mass for the Pope and Trees Have in Common

Who...Me?

After nine prayerful, awe-inspiring, and frankly, exhausting days in the Holy Land with my twenty-six fellow pilgrims, I had expected that my six days in Rome would be fairly laid back and less overwhelming. Boy, was I was wrong! When it first became official that my brother seminarians and I were going to be serving at the Papal Christmas Eve Mass, my initial reaction was a mixture of "Is this for real?" and, "I'm not worthy to do this!" Having the privilege to meet Pope Francis and assist him in the liturgy was the icing on the cake of my Christmas break. In the midst of all the excitement and anxiousness over the once-in-a-lifetime opportunity, and after the experience was over, the question that the other seven seminarians and I kept asking ourselves was, "Why us?" How did six guys from You've-never-heard-of-it, Illinois, one from Evansville, and one from Cincinnati merit an invitation to be a part of such an important celebration? The answer is: we didn't.

We Aren't Worthy of Anything

During and after the Mass, I reflected on my unworthiness to travel to the Holy Land, to attend Masses at the holiest places on earth, (from the cave where Christ was born to the tomb where he was buried and resurrected), and to serve at a Papal Mass. I immediately perceived a parallel between my own unworthiness in these special circumstances and the unworthiness that we all share as human beings in everyday life. None of us, not even the greatest saint who ever lived, has done anything to merit our being created, our continued existence, and our redemption. As Saint Paul wrote, "...all have sinned and fall short of the glory of God" (Rm 3:23). In fact, the whole story of our existence is complete unworthiness being met by incomprehensible Love—from the Fall of our parents Adam and Eve and our own sinfulness to the total self-sacrifice of Jesus Christ in his Passion and Death. The truth is, if you're waiting until you feel worthy before you act on what you perceive to be God's will for your life, then you'll never move!

A Drop in the Ocean of God's Blessings

In our fast-paced, noisy, and image-saturated modern world, the vast majority of us (myself included) have a severely underdeveloped sense of wonder. We are taught from a young age to get excited about the "next big thing," be that a new gadget, clothing style, car, music album, film, you name it. While none of these things are necessarily evil in themselves, they often rob us of our childlike sense of wonder and curiosity towards natural beauty. The Christmas Mass was absolutely beautiful. St. Peter's Basilica, the decorations, the vestments, the liturgy, the music— everything was beautiful and in its proper place. While keeping all of this in mind (if that's even possible), I was later considering the beauty of a single tree. (Next time you're outside near a tree, just stop and look at it more closely). Consider the way its roots plunge deep into the ground, reaching out to scavenge for vital resources, the roughness and shape of the bark that protects it from insects and harsh elements, the strength of its branches, which reach up into the sky like arms towards their Creator, and the soft yet durable leaves through which the plant regularly performs feats of chemistry so efficient that our best scientists cannot even dream of replicating them in a state-of-the-art laboratory. This tree, along with the trillions upon trillions of other plants in the world, are constantly carrying out the photosynthesis that produces the oxygen necessary for our survival. The question is, what did we do to deserve this? Nothing. What's my point? We are infinitely more worthy to meet any famous person, visit any site, or participate in any event then we are to receive any of the countless blessings that are constantly being communicating to us at any given moment in our lives. The difference is, our hearts are fickle, and we quickly become complacent and take for granted all the tremendous blessings in our lives, which are right in front of our eyes at every moment. Hopefully, it doesn't take something such as serving for the Pope for us to realize this great truth!

Serving at the Papal Christmas Eve Mass was, to be sure, a totally unexpected and inspiring experience, and one that I will forever remember and treasure in my heart. However, what's even more amazing is the gift to be sitting here at my laptop right now, still existing, taking another breath, and having the opportunity to live another moment doing whatever I choose to do for the glory of God.

> ...let the peace of Christ rule in your hearts, to which indeed you were called in the one body. And be thankful. Let the word of Christ dwell in you richly, teach and admonish one another in all wisdom, and sing psalms and hymns and spiritual songs with thankfulness in your hearts to God. And whatever you do, in word or deed, do everything in the name of the Lord Jesus, giving thanks to God the Father through him (Col 3:15-17).

Don't Wait!

Whenever we feel unworthy to receive God's gifts or to be used by him, let us remember who Jesus founded his Church on—a sinful, impulsive, and uneducated fisherman. Rather than listening to the lies of Satan and the world, which tell us that we aren't good enough and would have us believe that greatness is something we're born with, let us instead respond to the call of Christ the way Peter did:

> "Depart from me, for I am a sinful man, O Lord." For he was astonished, and all that were with him, at the catch of fish which they had taken...And Jesus said to Simon, "Do not be afraid; henceforth you will be catching men." And when they had brought their boats to land, they left everything and followed him. (Lk 5:8-11).

Let us pray to Jesus, that he may give us the grace to leave everything behind, not necessarily all of our material possessions and relationships like the apostles had to, but above all, our preconceptions, doubts, fears, and sinfulness, and follow him. God Bless you, and Merry Christmas!

† Under the Mercy,

Chris Trummer

Your god is Too Boring: Thoughts on Modern Paganism

Saint Maximilian Kolbe was a Catholic priest who voluntarily took the place of a man sentenced to die in a starvation chamber in Auschwitz. Why did he do it? Was he just a mindless, religious fanatic who had a silly belief that an "invisible man in the sky" would reward him for his sacrifice? Not hardly. Kolbe was a brilliant and well-educated man who had doctorate degrees in both philosophy and theology, and was fluent in several languages. He was also a master at utilizing the latest mass media tools of his time for the evangelization of the Catholic Faith. Like all of the Christian martyrs throughout history, Maximilian Kolbe had tapped into something real, something about which he had no doubts whatsoever. His faith underwent the ultimate test. C.S. Lewis summarized this test of faith in a brilliant way:

> You never know how much you really believe anything until its truth or falsehood becomes a matter of life and death to you. It is easy to say you believe a rope to be strong and sound as long as you are merely using it to cord a box. But suppose that you had to hang by that rope over a precipice. Wouldn't you then first discover how much you really trusted it? Only a real risk tests the reality of a belief (*A Grief Observed*).

The Epidemic

One of the great tragedies of our time is a widespread epidemic of boredom. We moderns have filled virtually every second of our day with some form of entertainment or stimuli, and yet, when you look around at peoples' faces, what do you see? Bored, stressed, anxious, and dissatisfied looks. Why? Because the average person in our society has enough money and resources to make life safe, planned, and predictable, and therefore boring. As Peter Kreeft wrote: The most total opposite of pleasure is not pain but boredom, for we are willing to risk pain to make a boring life interesting (*Jesus Shock*). The title of this post, "Your God is Too Boring," comes from my observations about the hobbies, interests, and religious attitudes of many people I meet, especially my peers. The typical teenager or young adult in our society has the primary interests of following sports, watching TV shows, listening to music (not the music of Bach or Mozart), drinking/partying, and "hooking up" with members of the opposite sex. In contrast to the gospel invitation of Jesus Christ, all of these are sad and boring alternatives (I know from experience). Instead of encouraging people to get outside of themselves, inviting them take the exciting risk of giving their entire life to something bigger than themselves (which they deeply long for), all of these alternatives turn the person inward, trapping them in a prison of egotism, self-centeredness, and comparison. I say "Your God is too boring" to these people (not literally) because any amount of time spent outside of their mindset reveals it to be painfully dull. Take following professional sports for example (I understand that many people reading this are probably huge sports fans, but please hear me out). Following a sports team to such an extent that your happiness and mood on a given day is tied up with the success or failure of "your" team seems very foolish to me. Why should I ground my happiness in something that is completely outside of my control? How does a bad call made by some referee actually impact my life in any way whatsoever? It doesn't! How many people waste their lives away watching other people play sports instead of enjoying the sports themselves? The most fun that some people have is watching other people have fun.

Everybody Worships

Now, in what sense are these hobbies or interests "gods?" They are for the following reasons. Human beings are naturally inclined to worship something. Like thirsting for water, being hungry for food, or craving sleep, we all have an innate desire to worship, praise, and thank something or someone greater than ourselves. Anytime we don't choose God as the object of this desire, we immediately replace Him with some lesser object (By object I mean 'source of fulfillment,' not merely a 'thing'). As Kreeft wrote, "The opposite of theism is not atheism, but the worship of a false god!" Soren Kierkegaard wrote, "Sin is building your identity and life on anything other than God." Saint Paul perhaps said it best of all in his letter to the Romans, referring to the pagans:

86

...although they knew God they did not honor him as God or give thanks to him, but they became futile in their thinking and their senseless minds were darkened. Claiming to be wise, they became fools...they exchanged the truth about God for a lie and worshiped and served the creature rather than the Creator, who is blessed for ever! (Rm 1:21-22,25).

In light of this wisdom, we can see clearly that, especially in our modern society of rampant consumerism, there is not so much widespread secularism as there is widespread paganism. Instead of saints, we venerate actors, actresses, musicians, and athletes; instead of holiness and virtue, we aspire to success and material wealth; instead of cathedrals, we build stadiums; instead of cherishing the joy of the Christmas season, we cherish the deals of the Christmas season, instead of attending the Mass, we attend "the game."

What Has Your god Done?

What can be said on behalf of these false gods? Your god sold the most albums in 2014, my God has sold the most book copies in the history of the world; your god created a Super Bowl winning team out of unlikely players, my God created a two-thousand-year-old Church out of a dozen uneducated fishermen; your god broke the record for home runs in a season, my God breaks the hardened hearts of all who seek Him; your god is your favorite food, my God gives Himself as food for me; your god wrote a New York Times best-seller, my God wrote the Laws of Nature; your god is responsible for the death of millions of innocent people, my God is responsible for the redemption of every person who ever lived and ever will live; your god denies the humanity of an unborn child, my God took on the humanity of an unborn child; your god founded the most profitable organization on the planet, my God founded the most charitable organization on the planet.

What Do You Seek?

If you're bored with God, then it's not God you're dealing with but a caricature of your own creation or choosing. If you don't recognize

Jesus Christ as the answer, then it's because you still haven't found the question. When Jesus met two of the disciples of John the Baptist, he asked them, "What do you seek?" (Jn 1:38). When they responded by asking him, "Teacher, where are you staying?" he answered, "Come and see" (1:38-39). Will you come and see the God who puts hymns on the lips of martyrs? Or will you be content to sacrifice all of your time and energy to the false gods of this world on the altar of your own comfort zone? Let us all resolve to make the one true God the center of our lives, and to "not be conformed this world but be transformed by the renewal of [our] minds" (Rom 12:2). Thank you for reading, and may God bless you!

† Under the Mercy,

Chris Trummer

Confession: The Line I Enjoy Waiting In

Why the Empty Boxes?

No, I'm not talking about the line at the DMV, or the lunch line at school. I'm talking about the line to the confessional in Church. Unfortunately, the Sacrament of Penance, which today is more commonly referred to as the Sacrament of Confession or Reconciliation, has become greatly under-appreciated and under-used by Catholics, and so it's rare that I get the opportunity to wait in this line. According to a national survey conducted at Georgetown University, three out of four Catholics report going to confession less than yearly or not at all. Also, just 2 percent report going at least once a month. Years ago (50+), the lines at the confessionals were long in virtually every Church anytime the Sacrament was offered, which was then (and still is today) typically on Saturdays in most parishes, and on additional days in a few parishes. There are several possible explanations or causes for this relatively rapid and recent decline in the number of Catholics who make use of the Sacrament of Confession. Here I list them in order from what I consider to be the least likely and apparent causes to those most probable and apparent.

1) A decrease in the commission of serious sins by Catholics in recent years
2) A change in the Catholic Church's teaching about the necessity or importance of the Sacrament of Penance
3) A cultural shift in how people understand sin, guilt, and personal accountability
4) Confusion and misunderstanding about the nature and purpose of the Sacrament, resulting from poor or even non-existent catechesis on the matter

Sin is Still "In"

If you were hoping that I would consider the first possibility as a valid explanation for the decline in Catholic practice of Confession, please turn on the news for ten minutes, walk outside your front door, or make a brief examination of your own conscience! Sin has not become any less popular during the last fifty years. In fact, it has been "in fashion" since Satan first sold the idea to Adam and Eve. Many people, especially those who do not make use of the Sacrament of Confession, would probably cite the second reason I listed as a likely explanation for the empty confessional boxes. This view is tempting, because if true, it would seem to let Catholics "off the hook" ("If the Church doesn't think confession is important, why should I?"). The problem with this view is that, like other problems in the Church which people try to blame on the Church herself, it is simply not accurate at all. "But Chris," someone might ask, "what about Vatican II, didn't it do away with all of the superstition, scrupulosity, and harsh judgmental attitudes that made people feel guilty enough need to go to Confession every week?" As a general rule, anytime a person tries to justify their view with a vague appeal to the teaching of the Second Vatican Council, it's usually wrong. In fact, this general rule applies not only to the teachings of the Vatican II, but to all of the teachings of the Catholic Church. If we want to know what the Church teaches about something, we should always first look to the Church herself and what she has officially taught (e.g., by consulting her Catechism), rather than allowing ourselves to be misled by potentially misinformed people or climates of opinion. In the case of a person referencing Vatican II, the only response that is usually necessary is to ask them, "Have you ever actually read the documents of Vatican II?" Nine times out of ten, the answer is, "Well, no..." (Sounds fair, right?). That being said, what did the Council teach about the Sacrament of Penance anyway? Here is a small sampling:

> Those who approach the sacrament of Penance obtain pardon from the mercy of God for the offence committed against Him and are at the same time reconciled with the Church, which they have wounded by their sins, and which by charity, example, and prayer seeks their conversion (Lumen Gentium).

> Pastors should [be] mindful of how much the sacrament of Penance contributes to developing the Christian life and, therefore, should always make themselves available to hear the confessions of the faithful (Christus Dominus).

In the spirit of Christ the Shepherd, [pastors] must prompt their people to confess their sins with a contrite heart in the sacrament of Penance, so that, mindful of his words "Repent for the kingdom of God is at hand" (Mt 4:17), they are drawn closer to the Lord more and more each day (Presbyterorum Ordinis).

What is Sin?

Seeing that the Second Vatican Council certainly did not "do away" with Confession in any sense, nor seek to downplay it's importance, we are left to conclude that the decline in the practice of confession among Catholics today must be the result of one or both of the last two possible causes. The prevalence of pop-psychology in our culture, of "I'm okay, you're okay" thinking and best-seller lists full of "self-help" books, is evidence that the third explanation is true, almost without question. Also, there is a widespread attitude of moral relativism in our society, which has sadly become the default view taught in the majority of our children's schools, TV shows, and in all forms of the media, from news to entertainment. My father always says, "The only sins that people believe in today are 'hurting someone's feelings' and 'judging people.'" Our current president articulated this relativistic attitude quite well when, in a 2008 interview for the Chicago Sun Times, he was asked what his definition of "sin" was and answered, "Being out of alignment with my values." In other words, when he sins, Barack Obama is offending himself and his own subjective standards of morality, not the God who created him and the objective moral values and duties that we all encounter every day of our lives. Unfortunately, it seems as though many Americans, if not most, would agree with Obama's definition of sin.

What is Confession?

The most manifest cause for confession-box-absenteeism is the fourth one that I listed – confusion and misunderstanding about the nature and purpose of the sacrament. There are numerous questions raised by people who don't properly understand what the Church teaches about the Sacrament of Confession, including:

What is Confession exactly?
Where is it taught in the Bible?
Why does the Church require it?
How can it possibly help me?
Why can't I just confess my sins directly to God instead of telling them to a priest?

The Sacrament of Confession, like all of the seven Sacraments that the Catholic Church offers, is an "...efficacious [sign] of grace, instituted by Christ and entrusted to the Church, by which divine life is dispensed to us" (CCC 1131). So, if Confession was instituted by Christ, when did he institute it and where is that institution in the Bible? It is most clear in the Gospel of John, when Jesus first appeared to the apostles after his Resurrection:

> On the evening of that day, the first day of the week, the doors being shut where the disciples were, for fear of the Jews, Jesus came and stood among them and said to them, "Peace be with you." When he had said this, he showed them his hands and his side. Then the disciples were glad when they saw the Lord. Jesus said to them again, "Peace be with you. As the Father has sent me, even so I send you." And when he had said this, he breathed on them, and said to them, "Receive the Holy Spirit. If you forgive the sins of any, they are forgiven; if you retain the sins of any, they are retained" (Jn 20:19-23).

"As the Father has sent me..." How did God the Father send Jesus? With "all authority in heaven and on earth" (Mt 28:18). "All authority" includes the authority to forgive sins. Remember the story about Jesus forgiving the paralytic?

> And getting into a boat he crossed over and came to his own city. And behold, they brought to him a paralytic, lying on his bed; and when Jesus saw their faith he said to the paralytic, "Take heart, my son; your sins are forgiven." And behold, some of the scribes said to themselves, "This man is blaspheming." But Jesus, knowing their thoughts, said, "Why do you think evil in your hearts? For which is easier, to say, 'Your sins are forgiven,' or to say, 'Rise and walk'? But that you may know that the

Son of man has authority on earth to forgive sins"—he then said to the paralytic—"Rise, take up your bed and go home" (Mt 9:1-7).

If you forgive the sins of any, they are forgiven; if you retain the sins of any, they are retained. How would the apostles know which sins to forgive and which to retain unless people first confessed them? We never read about Jesus giving the apostles the power to read minds!

Sin Can Be Personal, But Never Private

The question still remains, why did Jesus institute this Sacrament in the first place? Why not let people just keep their sins between them and God? Saint Paul provides the insight we need to answer these questions:

> For just as the body is one and has many members, and all the members of the body, though many, are one body, so it is with Christ. For by one Spirit we were all baptized into one body...If one member suffers, all suffer together; if one member is honored, all rejoice together (1 Cor 12:12-13, 26).

If one members suffers, all suffer together. Is there any greater suffering than that brought by sin? No, which is why when we sin, we seriously damage not only our own soul and relationship with God, but the entire Body of Christ. In the Sacrament of Penance, the priest is participating in the ministry of his bishop, who has inherited the authority given by Christ to the apostles to "forgive and retain" sins. When the priest grants a person absolution, he is not performing some action by his own power. Rather, he is serving as God's instrument to reconcile the person with Jesus Christ and his Body, the Church. The theology of this is clear when we read (or hear) the prayer of absolution:

> God the Father of Mercies, through the Death and Resurrection of His Son, has reconciled the world to Himself and sent the Holy Spirit among us for the forgiveness of sins. Through the ministry of the Church, may God grant you pardon and peace, and I absolve you of your sins, in the name of the Father, and of the Son, and of the Holy Spirit. Amen.

Even though the priest says, "I absolve you of your sins," he does not do so by his own power or authority, which is why he also says, "In the name of the Father, and of the Son, and of the Holy Spirit." The words, "In the name of" are equivalent to, "By the power/authority of." A modern example of this would be when a police officer yells at a fleeing criminal, "Stop in the name of the law!"

Just Following Orders Here!

Once we understand what sin is, how it affects us, and how it affects the entire Body of Christ, it is much easier to understand why Christ would leave us with the great gift that the Sacrament of Confession is, and why the Church in her wisdom would require all of her children to participate in that Sacrament at least once per year. The role of the Church is to nourish, teach, guide, and protect all of her members. To ignore the reality of sin, to downplay the power it has to damage individual souls and the overall health of the Body of Christ, would be a tragic form of neglect on the part of the Church. In offering the Sacrament of Confession to people, the Church is not undermining the role of Christ as Redeemer and Forgiver—she is obeying the command of Christ, who told his apostles to make disciples of all nations, "...teaching them to observe all that I have commanded you" (Mt 28:20). Is Confession comfortable? No, but if surgery of the body isn't comfortable, why should surgery of the soul be any different? I suspect that, more than anything else, the primary cause of the decline in practice of confession is the modern and typically American ideal, which falsely believes that "I am completely independent and self-sufficient, and I don't need other people judging me or telling me how to live my life." However, as the saying goes, "No man is an island," and if we cannot forgive others when they offend us, how can we expect to God to forgive us when we offend Him? The prayer that Jesus gave us, the Our Father, contradicts this, asking God to "forgive us our trespasses as we forgive those who trespass against us." In other words, we are God's standard for our own forgiveness.

Do You Come Here Often?

The reason why the line to confession is the one line that I enjoy waiting in is that, far from judging or thinking less of the other people in line with me, I greatly admire them! Nothing is more encouraging to me then to see my brothers and sisters in Christ striving in their faith, and being humble enough to admit your own sinfulness and brokenness is the first step to becoming a saint. Future saints make the best company! Thank you very much for taking the time to read this post. I'll leave you with this quote from a homily of one of my favorite priests, Father Mike Schmitz:

> When we go to Confession, we're not telling God something He doesn't already know, or showing Him something He doesn't already see. We're giving Him something He doesn't already have—our broken heart.

Whether it's been a day, a month, two years, or twenty years since your last Confession, I hope this post has helped you to better understand what the Catholic Church teaches about this Sacrament, and if you have felt up to this point that Confession wasn't for you for any reason, I invite you to prayerfully reconsider. May God Bless you!

† Under the Mercy,

Chris Trummer

Sources:

Catholic Biblical Association (Great Britain). *The Holy Bible: Revised Standard Version, Catholic Edition.* New York: National Council of Churches of Christ in the USA, 1994. Print.

Catholic Church. *Catechism of the Catholic Church.* 2nd Ed. Washington, DC: United States Catholic Conference, 2000. Print.

Catholic Church. "Decree Concerning the Pastoral Office of Bishops in the Church: Christus Dominus." *Vatican II Documents.* Vatican City: Libreria Editrice Vaticana, 2011. Print.

Catholic Church. "Decree on the Ministry and Life of Priests: Presbyterorum Ordinis." *Vatican II Documents.* Vatican City: Libreria Editrice Vaticana, 2011. Print.

Catholic Church. "Dogmatic Constitution on the Church: Lumen Gentium." *Vatican II Documents.* Vatican City: Libreria Editrice Vaticana, 2011. Print.

Schmitz, Michael, Rev. "UMD Newman Catholic Campus Ministry." 2014. Podcast.

A Homily of Beauty: Mass at the Sea of Galilee

The following is a reflection that I wrote during my pilgrimage to the Holy Land over Christmas break. It was written on December 16, 2014.

Yesterday I experienced more beauty than I have on any other day in my memory. I wasn't planning on even attempting to recount the day in words, but after further reflection, I felt an obligation to communicate at least something of my experience. Yesterday morning we had an outdoor Mass about 100 meters from the shore of the Sea of Galilee, outside of the Church of the Primacy of Peter in a miniature amphitheater. During Mass, the background was the same place where Jesus walked on water, where he appeared to the apostles after his Resurrection, and where he gave Peter the special responsibility of being the shepherd of his flock on earth. It was so surreal, powerful, mystical, amazing – I don't know what other words to say! Even Deacon Adam, who proclaimed the Gospel and preached, admitted that he was at a loss for words to give a substantial homily, which was probably for the best, because the overwhelming beauty and power of the moment would have drowned out any analytic or practical interpretation. When faced with such beauty, truth and goodness seem to be directly infused into the human soul, in a way that makes ordinary language and deliberate, logical thinking more of an obstacle than a help. In other words, the beauty of the place and the moment was a homily in itself. After Deacon Adam concluded his short homily and sat down, there was about thirty seconds of perfect silence. I say "perfect" silence and not "complete" silence because I think there is a significant difference between the two.

This silence was not artificial, such as the silence achieved by jamming ear plugs into one's ears, or like the lifeless and haunting vacuum that I imagine outer space must provide. This silence was full, beautiful, and complete. I can clearly remember sitting there thinking, "I could sit here like this forever." There were distant chirps of small birds and quiet rustlings in the trees from the wildlife. The breeze kissed my face in such a perfect way – it was as if each individual air molecule was a separate and intentional consolation sent by God. The smell of the Sea of Galilee was noticeable, but it was a fresh and inviting smell, not like the smell of the murky rivers and lakes in Illinois that I'm used to. The surface of the Sea provided a shimmering backdrop for the liturgy taking place in front of us. What touched me the most was that, in spite of all of this unfamiliar and jaw-dropping beauty around us, the moment when the beauty seemed to reach its climax was still during the elevation of the Host. When Father Bob lifted it, the light reflecting off the water shined through the leaves of the tree behind him and illumined the Host completely. It was as though everything was in its proper place: God's Creation proclaiming his glory, God's people worshipping Him, and God nourishing His people in the most intimate and powerful way possible. The natural beauty around me was not a distraction from the Divine Beauty in front of me, but was like a lovely picture frame. When you see the frame by itself, you think, "Wow, that frame looks gorgeous!" but when you're viewing a masterpiece painting housed inside the same frame, your focus is entirely on the painting. Natural beauty, having the Divine Artist as its source, does not reduce our appreciation for Divine Beauty, but enhances it, just as the words of a love poem enhance our appreciation for, not only language and poetry, but for the lover who wrote it.

One of my favorite elements of our Catholic Faith is that it is simply beautiful. Truth, goodness, and beauty are the three transcendentals that all of us human beings desire, and desire infinitely. Everything that I'm experiencing on this pilgrimage is revitalizing my appreciation of beauty, both natural and man-made. Whether it's mathematical, scientific, moral, or religious truth, we can recognize it most easily by its beauty and simplicity. Thanks be to God for giving all of us here the opportunity to deepen our faith by immersing ourselves in the beauty of the holy places where His Son Jesus Christ once walked. May we continue to experience the beauty, truth, and goodness of our Faith in the remaining days of this blessed adventure.

† Under the Mercy,

Chris Trummer

Abortion: The Worst Kind of Poverty

Since we are privileged enough to live in a country as wealthy and prosperous as the United States, it's easy for us to believe that we are truly rich, and that we have eradicated poverty for the most part in our society. Blessed Mother Teresa, who spent the majority of her life serving the poor, marginalized, diseased, and dying people of Calcutta in India, firmly disagreed with these preconceptions. In 1975, when an English interviewer expressed pity for the people she served, her response shocked him:

> The spiritual poverty of the Western World is much greater than the physical poverty of our people...You, in the West, have millions of people who suffer such terrible loneliness and emptiness. They feel unloved and unwanted. These people are not hungry in the physical sense, but they are in another way. They know they need something more than money, yet they don't know what it is. What they are missing, really, is a living relationship with God.

Having spent the majority of her life living among and serving people who experienced some of the worst physical suffering and deprivation possible, Mother Teresa was an authority on human suffering. Years after this interview, she would hear about the epidemic of abortion in the West, and famously comment, "It is a poverty to decide that a child must die so that you may live as you wish."

Abortion is NOT a Religious Issue

The vast majority of people who oppose abortion are religious, especially in the United States. Unfortunately, this fact leads many supporters of legalized abortion to assume that the only reason people oppose abortion is because it conflicts with their religious beliefs. While sincere religious belief, and belief in Christianity in particular, will certainly motivate a person to work more diligently in the cause of putting an end to abortion, it does not follow that the Pro-Life movement is a religious movement, or even that the best arguments for the Pro-Life view depend on a belief in

God or the Bible. On the contrary, it can be shown that abortion is a severe violation of basic human rights on the basis of ethical principals and medical science alone, apart from the revelation or teachings of any religious tradition. Therefore, the Pro-Life movement is a civil rights movement, not a religious movement, which is why there are secular and even atheist people who support it.

Every argument that I've ever heard or read in defense of legalized abortion either makes an irrelevant distinction between unborn and born children or else could also be used to justify infanticide.The following argument summarizes why abortion is immoral and should therefore not be lawful in any country that claims to respect human rights:

1. All human beings have the right to life.
2. Unborn children, regardless of their stage in development, are human beings.
3. Therefore, unborn children have the right to life.

"It's My Body!"

From the instant that the female's egg cell is fertilized by the male's sperm cell, a new, separate, and unique organism exists. Despite how much supporters of legalized abortion like to present themselves as being up-to-date scientifically speaking, many of them still either fail to recognize, or worse, refuse to accept this undisputed fact of biology. Ambiguous, inaccurate, or even blatantly false terms and phrases are often used in an attempt to redefine the newly formed human being as something else, such as: clump of tissue, collection of cells, pregnancy, potential human being, and parasite (yes, seriously). An organism is an individual living member of a species. A clump of cells, whether they make up a tumor or part of a human organ, will never grow into an adult member of the human species, like an embryo will under normal conditions. In short, everything that science tells us about human embryos and their development supports the idea that the life created at conception, while completely dependent on its mother for survival, is a unique and separate human organism, which, given time, nutrition, and the proper environment, will grow into a fully developed human being like you or I.

"Fetuses Aren't Human Beings"

Usually, when people try to argue that embryos or fetuses aren't human beings, they will point to some factor or set some criteria which they claim disqualifies the unborn life in the womb from being considered a human being. Such factors include: having the shape/form of a human being, having all of it's own functioning organs, viability (the ability to survive outside of the womb), and a nervous system capable of experiencing pain. The problem with all of these factors is that, when defining what is essential to being human, they are all irrelevant. Given how gradual the process of human development is, there is no concrete moment that you can point to as the moment in which the life form/organism becomes human. If the unborn are not human because of their level of development, then newborn children who are barely more developed should not be considered human beings either. Also, if consistently applied, this reasoning would also imply that no one is fully human until they are in their twenties and a physically mature adult, which is clearly absurd. The viability factor also doesn't work as a criteria for determining whether or not something (someone) is a human being or not, because it is very common for premature infants to require incubators and other life support for survival, and it would rightly be considered seriously wrong to kill one of them. Often people will say, "Yeah, but they're born already." So, being human depends on your location? If a baby is halfway out of the womb, is it only half human? I suspect the sad truth is that people think this way because when a fetus is dismembered inside of its mother's womb during an abortion, the process is more secretive and hidden from sight. Lastly, the distinction based on the ability to experience pain is yet another insufficient way of determining whether or not the unborn life is human or not. There are two basic reasons for thinking this: 1) We are not only human beings during the moments when we are experiencing pain, and 2) There are millions of non-human animals that do feel pain but are not given the right-to-life reserved to human beings.

The Role of Language

A few months ago, I found myself reading through the (dreaded) comment section of an online article about abortion. In the comments, a woman had tried to defend the idea that fetuses are human beings, but she was ganged up on by a few people in favor of legalized abortion. The comments of one man in particular struck me as astonishingly illogical. He wrote to her, "No, it is not a human being. It is a fetus. Understand? Words have meaning. Learn your words." Apart from being extremely condescending, his comment was completely irrelevant to the question of whether or not fetuses are human beings. What is a human being? It's an individual, living member of the human species. What is a fetus? It's an individual, living member of the human species in an early stage of its development. The fact that we use different terms for human beings depending on their age or stage in development does not in any way undermine the fact that they are a human being. Imagine someone arguing, "No, it is not a human being. It is a teenager. Understand? Words have meaning. Learn your words." Ridiculous!

"I Think Abortion is Wrong, But..."

How many times has someone told you that they are personally opposed to abortion, but they don't want to "impose their views" on someone else? I hear it all the time. The question that always immediately comes to my mind is, "Why doesn't anybody ever use that logic with any other moral issue?" In other words, what is it about abortion that makes people believe it to be seriously wrong and yet still think that it should be legal? There seems to be only one plausible reason for this distinction regarding abortion. Unlike other moral actions in question, abortion is based entirely on sex, more specifically, on the Modern idea that all people have the right to have as much sex as they want without commitment or consequences. Contraceptives are the most common means of trying to achieve a responsibility-free sex life, and abortion is simply back-up contraception. If personal pleasure and being in control of your life are your idols, your only absolutes in life, then eventually your conscience can become so decayed that you're willing to sacrifice anything in order to possess those idols, even the life of an innocent human being. When you consider how frail and broken the heart of a person must be in order to accept abortion as a morally acceptable action, it becomes easier to understand how Mother Teresa could say, "It is a poverty to decide that a child must die so that you may live as you wish." If love is the most valuable thing that we can ever give or receive in life, then being deprived of love to such an extent that you would choose or support abortion is literally the worst kind of poverty possible.

A Most Disturbing Trend

When you read about the worst crimes committed against human beings throughout history, and especially the large scale crimes of the 20th century like the Holocaust, you will see a trend in the way the people responsible for those crimes understood their victims. Every case involved the redefining of human beings as non-human or sub-human. On the day before the March for Life in DC this year, I had the privilege to visit the National Holocaust Museum. While I had already read a significant amount about the Holocaust, seeing the displays, videos, and pictures showing the horrors which took place less than 80 years ago was a chilling but much needed reminder for me of just how much evil and destruction we humans are capable of bringing about. There was one video in particular that deeply disturbed me. In it, members of the British military were liberating a concentration camp, and while there were a few surviving prisoners to rescue, the soldiers spent days burying all the bodies and remains of bodies. In fact, there were so many bodies that they had to dig mass graves and push the bodies in with a bulldozer. When I saw the heaping pile of hundreds of starved and disfigured human corpses, I immediately recalled images that I had seen of dumpsters full of aborted human fetuses and their remains.

The Tide is Turning

While we cannot forget the atrocity of abortion, with all of the death and suffering it has caused over the last four decades, it is important to remember that the Pro-Life cause is steadily overpowering it's opposition, the so-called "Pro-Choice" movement. According to a 2013 Gallup poll, 58% of adults in America believe that abortion should be illegal in "all" or "nearly all" circumstances, while just 39% believe it should be legal in all circumstances. Also, while the Pro-Choice movement claims to defend the view of women, only 40% of women in America identify as Pro-Choice, and 57% consider themselves to be Pro-Life. Millenials (aged 18-34) are the group most likely to think that abortion should be illegal in all circumstances. Also, in the past two decades, the number of abortion clinics in the US has gone from 2,176 in 1991 to 582 by the end of 2013. In other words, the Pro-Life movement is winning now, and winning the future as well. With the wisdom and witness of the Catholic Church as our guide and spearhead, we WILL abolish abortion in this country and in the world. Let us pray for the conversion of all those who support abortion, all the mothers who have ever had an abortion, all the fathers who encouraged or forced them to have it, all the doctors and nurses who work at abortion clinics, and above all, for the innocent and helpless victims of abortion, the unborn children themselves, who have been robbed of their most fundamental right, their right to life, as well as their chance to be loved in this life.

"Each of us is willed, each of us is loved, each of us is necessary."
—Pope Emeritus Benedict XVI

† Under the Mercy,

Chris Trummer

Help My Unbelief! Facing Doubt on the Journey of Faith

"Lord, if it is you, bid me come to you on the water." He said, "Come."
So Peter got out of the boat and walked on the water and came to Jesus;
but when he saw the wind, he was afraid, and beginning to sink he cried
out, "Lord, save me!" Jesus immediately reached out his hand and caught
him, saying to him, "O man of little faith, why did you doubt?" (Mt
28:31)

What is Doubt?

In our faith journey, we inevitably have some experience of doubt, of
uncertainty in our belief in some aspect of our faith, be it in our own
value, in Jesus Christ, or even in the very existence of God. We are often
tempted to think of doubt as weakness, worthy of shame, or even sinful.
However, all of these are false understandings of doubt. Many of the
greatest saints throughout history experienced times of intense doubt and
even unbelief. Even people who believed in Jesus' power to heal and who
encountered him directly still felt doubt. In the Gospel of Mark, for
example, the father who brings his possessed son to Jesus to be healed
says to him,"I believe; help my unbelief!" (Mk 9:24). Realizing that
people with tremendous faith still experience doubt, what does doubt tell
us about our own faith?

First of all, doubt indicates that our faith is maturing, that we are
integrating the faith which most of us received as children into our adult
thinking and acting. When Jesus taught that we must become like a child
in order to enter the kingdom of God (Mt 18:3), he meant that we must
have the humility of a child, by admitting that we are not self-sufficient
and we depend on God for literally everything. He was not telling us
toreason like a child, as Saint Paul made clear in his first letter to the
Corinthians: "When I was a child, I spoke like a child, I thought like a
child, I reasoned like a child; when I became a man, I gave up childish
ways" (1 Cor 13:11). We all experienced the physical, emotional, and
psychological development that took place during our transition from
childhood to adulthood. Our spiritual development involves a similar
transition. There is a process that must take place if our faith is to evolve

from the cooperative faith of a child into the integrated faith of an adult. That process varies significantly from person to person, but the road to our mature faith is never completely straight and smooth. There are potholes, curves, twists, steep hills, and severe weather conditions along the way. Some of us may even look up to see that we have run off the road completely. In our darkest moments we may ask ourselves, "Where am I going? Do I even have a destination? What is the point of this journey?" This is doubt: anything that causes us to lose sight of who we are, who God is, or what He wants for us. If the doubt we're feeling is particularly severe, we may even stop believing in God for a time. This is commonly referred to as a "crisis of faith." It is rightly considered a crisis, because it is the collapse of the existential foundation of a person. If our faith is real, and it penetrates all the dimensions of our life, then the loss of that faith indeed constitutes a tragedy of monumental proportion.

What Causes Doubt?

What is the cause of doubt then? There are two primary causes of doubt: a lack of knowledge and a lack of faith.* A lack of knowledge is increasingly common, especially in recent times when religious education has been, to put it nicely, far from optimal. If we have confused or mistaken views about the Christian faith, then it cannot provide us with the consolation and hope that we need to endure the various trials of life. For example, if we believe that as Christians we must hold to a strictly literal interpretation of the book of Genesis in regards to Creation, then we are likely to see the discoveries of the natural sciences as detrimental to our faith. However, as we learn more about the proper way to read and interpret the Bible, which includes taking into account literary genre, style, and techniques, we see that there is no contradiction between scientific knowledge and revealed knowledge. The Bible only contradicts science when you try to read it as a science textbook, which it was never intended to be.

* By "faith" here I am referring to the theological virtue of faith in God, not merely the cognitive act of believing a particular proposition, e.g., "I have faith that Jesus Christ rose from the dead.".

A lack of faith is also common. If we lack faith, we are not necessarily confused about the nature of God, or hung up about an apparent contradiction in Scripture. Rather, we may simply feel unable to be convinced by what faith proposes to us. In other words, we sincerely desire to believe, but we can't will ourselves to do so. Maybe you find yourself in this position. Maybe the idea that there is an all-powerful, all-knowing, and all-loving God who created this mind blowing universe and yet still loves you so much that He became a human being and died to redeem you seems way too good to be true. Maybe you've cried in prayer and felt like God wasn't even there; maybe you've sat in Mass, watched the priest elevate the Host and felt nothing; maybe you've struggled with the same sins for years and you've given up hope that you can ever be free. If any of this resonates with you, then guess what? You have a lot in common with some of the greatest Christians who ever lived! Saint John of the Cross wrote a spiritual masterpiece based on the feeling that God has withdrawn from you (The Dark Night of the Soul). Blessed Mother Teresa, who experienced Christ in a direct and personal way (He spoke to her multiple times during her youth), said that she felt an intense spiritual "dryness"—an absence of consolation and feeling of God's presence—for more than forty years! The feeling that God has abandoned you is also brought out countless times in Sacred Scripture, especially in the Psalms:

> I said to myself in my good fortune:
> Nothing will ever disturb me.
> Your favor had set me on a mountain fastness,
> then you hid your face and I was put to confusion (Psalm 30).

Once understood, the theology of this is profound and beautiful, even if it seems troublesome at first. If God knows and loves us, and if He wants us to know and love Him, then why would He allow us to be "put to confusion," to experience doubt, and to even doubt His very existence? When we pray, our natural expectation is that we will receive some feeling of consolation, some sense of peace and comfort as a result. There is nothing wrong with this expectation, and most of the time we do experience at least some consolation whenever we pray. However, if we always experience positive feelings when we pray, then we become at risk of praying just to experience those feelings. In other words, we may start loving God for what He gives us instead of loving God for who He is. This disordering of our desires in prayer can damage our relationship with God, by making us begin to think that we can control or manipulate God in some way, which is unreasonable, unloving, and unjust. God usually provides us with plenty of consolation early on in our spiritual journey—He knows that we need it (Like a young child who will only behave well in exchange for a piece of candy or other reward). Once we have established a relationship of trust with God, He begins to periodically withdraw His consolation, to test how pure our love for Him is. This ensures that our love for God is properly ordered, that is, that we are loving Him above all other things, even ourselves. At this point, someone might object, "But if God is all-knowing, then doesn't He already know how pure our love for Him is, and how much testing our faith can handle?" Indeed, He does—but we don't. Think of Abraham. God knew that Abraham's faith was strong enough that he would be willing to sacrifice his only son, Isaac, out of pure obedience—but Abraham didn't know that. Once he knew what his faith could endure, he was prepared to carry out God's plan for his life with the bold confidence he would need. While the testing of our faith probably won't be quite as dramatic as it was for Abraham, we can experience the same transformative effects that he did if we respond with complete openness and trust.

Consider Christ

Jesus himself, while he is God and therefore could never doubt God in the normal sense of the word, did experience doubt in his human nature, and at times, even appeared to feel distant from God. This was certainly the case during his agony in the garden at Gethsemane, we he said, "Father, if thou art willing, remove this cup from me; nevertheless not my will, but thine, be done" (Lk 22:42). Being fully God and fully man, Jesus had doubts about what he was capable of enduring in his human body. Those feelings reached their climax as he was dying on the cross: "My God, my God, why hast thou forsaken me?" (Mt 27:46) Being one with God the

Father, Jesus was never actually forsaken or abandoned by Him. However, in order for his sacrifice to be total, Jesus had to experience not only physical suffering, but mental suffering as well. Anyone who has suffered from severe depression, anxiety, or other mental disorders knows that the mental aguish of conditions such as these can at times feel much worse than physical suffering (mental suffering is the cause of far more suicides than any physical suffering). It's relatively easy to maintain a spirit of acceptance and trust when you have the flu or a broken arm, but it's nearly impossible during a panic attack. That is why much attention and healing is needed for those who suffer from mental and nervous disorders; such people are more susceptible to doubt and at higher risk of despairing. The worst suffering isn't always visible, but that doesn't mean it should go unnoticed. This is why we must always be attentive to our brothers and sisters, and do our best to understand their struggles and needs. There is more to every person than what meets the eye. As Saint John Paul II once said, "They try to understand me from the outside, but I can only be understood from the inside." That being said, if we are struggling with something, we can't blame other people for not understanding if we won't let them inside. Knowing about a person can be one-sided, but actually knowing a person is always mutual.

An Invitation to Trust

When we experience doubt, it's not a sign that we're doing something wrong. In fact, it can often be a sign that we're doing something right. Doubt tells us that our faith is not merely the creative product of our own wishful thinking, but a priceless gift that is worth having tested and purified of all imperfect desires and motivations.

> In this you rejoice, though now for a little while you may have to suffer various trials, so that the genuineness of your faith, more precious than gold which though perishable is tested by fire, may redound to praise and glory and honor at the revelation of Jesus Christ (1 Pet 1:6-7).

The Lover demands the perfection of the beloved. Each time our faith is tested and we are tempted to doubt is a direct invitation from God to trust

Him. With the help of God's grace, let us resolve to do our best to always accept that invitation, recognizing that our faith in Him is not some "thing" that we can simply "lose," but rather a conscious decision to continue trusting a real Person, and to continue believing that our deepest desire has a fulfillment. If you are experiencing doubts about your faith or about God, resolve to take small, concrete steps to learn more about your faith and to grow closer to God. Seemingly insignificant practices, such as 5-10 minutes of reading Scripture each day, a silent drive in the car instead of a noise-filled one, and attending Mass just one extra time during the week, are actually powerful exercises of the will that remove distractions and obstacles, and enable us to a encounter God in a more intimate way. Another avenue is to improve your understanding of your faith by reading books that explain it. I highly recommend the works of C.S. Lewis, Peter Kreeft, Fr. Robert Spitzer, and Scott Hahn as good places to begin. Lastly, never underestimate the power of memory. If you feel distant from God, take time to reflect on the times in your past when you experienced Him in a powerful way. Reflect on the joy and life that those experiences brought you. You'll be surprised at the sustaining effect this can have. Memory is the uniquely human power to make the past present again.

May God bless you and draw you closer to Himself, so that your trust in Him may grow, giving you the strength to endure times of uncertainty, trial, and temptation. Thank you for reading!

† Under the Mercy,

Chris Trummer

The Historical Fact of the Resurrection

"Put your finger here, and see my hands; and put out your hand, and place it in my side; do not be faithless, but believing" (Jn 20:27).

When discussing matters of religion, whether philosophical ideas, theological doctrines, Biblical stories, spiritual charisms, prayer styles, or other related topics, it's easy to begin to think of religion as abstract or distant—something too mysterious and lofty to even approach. This is what makes Christianity so different from every other religion. Unlike many other mainstream religions, which are founded primarily on self-help psychology and superstitious speculation, the credibility of the Christian faith is based entirely on concrete and radical historical claims. The most central of all of these claims is the resurrection of Jesus Christ from the dead. Regarding the centrality of the Resurrection of Christ to the Christian faith, Saint Paul wrote the following:

> If Christ has not been raised, your faith is futile and you are still in your sins. Then those also who have fallen asleep in Christ have perished. If for this life only we have hoped in Christ, we are of all men most to be pitied (1 Cor 15:17-19).

Why would the Christian faith be "futile" though? Couldn't we still learn morals and practical life advice from the teachings of Jesus? Wouldn't Christianity still be important as an ideology or cause for good in the world today? Pope Emeritus Benedict XVI answered these questions in his second volume of Jesus of Nazareth:

> If [the Resurrection] were taken away, it would still be possible to piece together from the Christian tradition a series of interesting ideas about God and men, about man's being and his obligations, a kind of religious world view: but the Christian faith itself would be dead. Jesus would be a failed religious leader, who despite his failure remains great and can cause us to reflect. But he would then remain purely human, and his authority would extend only so far as his message is of interest to us. He would no longer be a criterion; the only criterion left would be our own

judgment in selecting from his heritage what strikes us as helpful. In other words, we would be alone (Ratzinger 241-242).

The resurrection of Jesus Christ from the dead is not one "doctrine" among other doctrines. It is not a nice "bonus" to the Gospel message or a kind of theological "icing-on-the-cake." The Resurrection is everything. It is the divine seal of credibility regarding the claims Jesus of Nazareth, proving both his divinity and consequently the divine authority of all his teachings. Recognizing that Jesus' resurrection is the foundation of our Christian faith, the question is this: How do we know that it's true? How do we know Jesus actually rose from the dead? Are there convincing historical and logical reasons for believing in the Resurrection? Or do we simply have to accept it as a matter of faith? What reasons might non-Christians offer for not believing in the Resurrection?

Miracle Haters Gonna Hate Miracles

To begin, a more foundational objection to the truth of the Resurrection must be set aside, and that is objecting to the Resurrection simply because it is a miraculous event. This objection is not a historical or scientific one, but a philosophical one; it is the rejection of any supernatural intervening into the natural realm, or, more fundamentally, the rejection of the supernatural altogether. The problem with this objection is that it is immune to being disproven on the basis of solid evidence, and instead dismisses all evidence that could potentially disprove it as non-evidence on the basis of the objector's preconceptions, personal desires, or other biases. It effectively says, "The Resurrection could not have happened, because it would be a miracle, and miracles can't happen." This is begging the question. The question that must be answered is not whether or not miracles can occur, but whether or not the Resurrection did in fact occur. If it did, then the answer to the question of whether or not miracles can occur is, "Yes."

112

What Needs to Be Explained?

With this in mind, we must first consider the basic facts of history, which come from both the New Testament and non-Christian sources (Roman and Jewish historians), in order to establish what exactly needs to be explained. It is not necessary to presuppose the documents of the New Testament as infallible or even true in order to establish basic historical facts regarding the events surrounding the death of Jesus of Nazareth. These facts are not based on belief in Christianity, God, or even the existence of a supernatural reality. Any alternative theory to the actual resurrection of Jesus Christ from the dead would have to explain all of the following data:

– Jesus' death by crucifixion
– The discovery of the empty tomb
– The post-mortem appearances of Jesus to numerous people
– The faith of the early Christians (not the truth of it, but the existence of it)

The Options

There are four possible alternative explanations or theories to account for these facts besides the Christian belief in the Resurrection, all of which have been believed and argued by various people throughout history. If all the alternative explanations to the actual resurrection of Jesus can be disproven (or shown to be highly implausible), then the most reasonable explanation of the above data is Christianity. In the words of Sherlock Holmes, "When you have eliminated the impossible, whatever remains, however improbable, must be the truth." The alternative possibilities to the actual resurrection of Jesus Christ include:

1. The Swoon Theory
2. The Hallucination Theory
3. The Conspiracy Theory
4. The Myth Theory

Resurrection or Recovery?

The "Swoon" theory claims that Jesus was crucified, taken down from the cross, and laid in the tomb, but that he never actually died and only appeared to be dead (he "swooned"). After being laid in the tomb, Jesus was later helped out of it by some other person or persons, and once nursed back to health, returned to his apostles and other followers. The first problem with this theory is that Roman crucifixion, even without the additional scourging and physical trauma that Christ suffered, was designed to kill people. Crucifixion was a common form of the death penalty, and so Roman soldiers were quite efficient at "getting the job done," so to speak. Secondly, the Jewish people had a constant and intimate experience of dealing with the bodies of dead people, due to their very involved burial traditions and rituals. This means that they would have been familiar with what a dead person feels and looks like. It is highly improbable that both the expert Roman executioners and the Jews who buried Jesus would have mistaken him for being dead. Also, even if he had been so close to dying that he was mistaken for being dead, he could not have survived for long after being buried, and certainly not lying in a tomb deprived of water and serious medical attention. An additional proof that Jesus actually died comes from the Gospel of John, when one of the soldiers pierced the side of Christ and "at once there came out blood and water" (Jn 19:34). This is evidence of an actual medical phenomenon known as "pericardial effusion," in which fluid (mostly water) builds up around the heart. The fact that both blood and water came out when Christ's side was pierced is evidence that the soldier's spear actually hit his heart, which definitely would have killed him if he were somehow still alive at that point. A final and very compelling objection to the Swoon theory is that it does not explain the faith of the early Christians. Would you be convinced or motivated by seeing the man who you believed to be your Savior limping around half-alive? Probably not. It also doesn't explain why the early Christians believed that Jesus died on the cross, or why there is no record of Jesus dying at a later date.

Were the Apostles Just "Tripping?"

The Hallucination theory claims that Jesus died on the cross and was buried, but that instead of rising from the dead, he appeared to his followers as some sort of hallucination or product of their imaginations. The first problem is the empty tomb; if Jesus didn't actually rise from the dead, and his followers were simply deceived into thinking he did, then what happened to his body? Did the apostles take it from the tomb? That is extremely unlikely, because how could the same group of people simultaneously know that Jesus was still dead and believe their hallucinations to the contrary? And who else would have wanted to steal Jesus' body (at the risk of severe punishment or death, since the tomb was guarded)? If the apostles had gone around claiming that Jesus rose from the dead, both the Jewish and Roman authorities could have easily went to his tomb and disproven their claim. The next problem is the greater one, namely, the very idea of a group of individuals sharing a collective hallucination. The problem with this concept is that there is absolutely no psychological evidence whatsoever that collective hallucination is even possible—hallucinations are rare and private events. Even if we allow for some sort of group hallucination, how long could that possibly last? A few minutes? A few hours? Highly unlikely. But forty days? Impossible. Additionally, the accounts of Jesus' appearances include him interacting with the apostles and the world in physical ways, which a hallucination obviously could not do. Because he knew their doubts, the resurrected Jesus insists that his apostles physically touch him (Lk 24:39), and he eats food (Lk 24:42-43). The apostles might have initially thought they were hallucinating, but Jesus went out of his way to prove otherwise.

It's a Conspiracy, Man!

The Conspiracy theory claims that Jesus did not rise from the dead, but that his resurrection was the deliberate invention of his followers. There are numerous problems with this theory. The theory claims that a small group of simple Jewish fisherman not only came up with the most radical lie in all of human history, but that they were all willing to die for that lie and were able to convince thousands of other people to be willing do die for it as well. It is perhaps conceivable that extremely depressed and fanatical disciples might contrive of such a grande scheme regarding their recently killed leader, but what could their motivations have been for doing so? Liars (not insane people, but liars) always have some selfish motivation or agenda. One would think that if this were the case with the apostles, then the first beheading, boiling alive, or crucifixion of one of their comrades would have been enough to make them spill the beans. That's the problem with liars—they make terrible martyrs. Another problem with the Conspiracy theory is that, given the Jewish theological beliefs and expectations of the apostles, it is unthinkable that they could conceive of the idea of Christ's resurrection, much less do so in a way that would convince countless other Jews of a similar mindset. It is important to realize that, while many Jews believed in a bodily resurrection of the dead, they only believed in that regarding the end of time. This is why, when Jesus told her that her brother Lazarus would rise, Martha responded, "I know that he will rise again in the resurrection at the last day" (Jn 11:24). The idea that someone could die and rise before the end of time was totally foreign to Jews. Another issue comes from the Gospels and other New Testament writings. In the Gospels, any time people are confronted with the idea that Jesus has risen from the dead, their initial response is almost always one of confusion and disbelief. The most famous example of this is the apostle Thomas, or "doubting Thomas" as he is often called. Recall Thomas' response to hearing of Jesus' resurrection:

> Now Thomas, one of the twelve, called the Twin, was not with them when Jesus came. So the other disciples told him, "We have seen the Lord." But he said to them, "Unless I see in his hands the print of the nails, and place my finger in the mark of the nails, and place my hand in his side, I will not believe (Jn 20:24-25).

The question is this: If you were trying to create a false narrative about a man who rose from the dead, and wanted everyone to believe your story, why would you include multiple instances of people doubting that story? There are several other documented cases of people doubting the reality of Jesus' resurrection: The apostles listening to the testimony of Mary

Magdalene and the other women (Lk 24:10-11), Mary Magdalene herself near the tomb (Jn 20:14), the disciples on the road to Emmaus (Lk 24:13-35), and a group of the apostles by the Sea of Tiberius (Jn 21:12). The only reasonable explanation for including stories in which people doubt the resurrection of Jesus is that they are actually true. There is a similar argument to be made from the fact that it was women who first discovered the empty tomb of Jesus. Unfortunately, the culture in that place and time was such that the testimony of a woman carried no weight in any official or legal sense. Therefore, if you were trying to convince the people in that culture to believe in the resurrection of Jesus, then having women as some of your primary witnesses would be a really poor strategy. If you're making up the story, why not have a few members of the Jewish Sanhedrin (the group that condemned Jesus to death) be the first ones to discover the empty tomb? The most reasonable explanation for why women are said to be the first witnesses of the resurrection is—they were. What all of these examples tell us is that if the apostles of Jesus were trying to make up an account of the resurrection that would convince the people of their time (especially the Jews) then they did a really lousy job!

Jesus Christ: The Man, or the Myth and the Legend?

The Myth theory is probably the most subtle of all the alternative explanations to the resurrection of Jesus. The Myth theory claims that the resurrection of Jesus was not a deliberate conspiracy of the apostles or other followers of him, but that the idea developed slowly over time amongst the early Christians. The plausibility of the Myth theory is largely dependent on the idea that the Gospels and other New Testament documents were written much later then what is traditionally believed. The reason for this is that myths take multiple generations to develop, because new ideas about a person, event, or story cannot be introduced while witnesses to the contrary are still alive and able to testify against them. Saint Paul himself makes this clear in his first letter to the Corinthians:

> For I delivered to you as of first importance what I also received, that Christ died for our sins in accordance with the scriptures, that he was

buried, that he was raised on the third day in accordance with the scriptures, and that he appeared to Cephas, then to the twelve. Then he appeared to more than five hundred brethren at one time, most of whom are still alive, though some have fallen asleep (1 Cor 15:3-6).

He writes, "most of whom are still alive" as a way of saying, "Go ask them yourselves if you don't believe me!" The effort of so-called "de-mythologizing" was especially prevalent during the early and mid-20th century, which made the Myth theory of the Resurrection seem more plausible to many people. However, the historical-critical method also became more popular during this time, and aided by the discovery of the Dead Sea Scrolls (older manuscripts of Biblical texts), it provided solid confirmation of the original dating of the Gospels and other New testament documents. This confirmation dated the Gospel of Luke and the letters of Saint Paul (e.g. Romans, Corinthians 1 and 2, etc.) as being prior to the destruction of Jerusalem (70 A.D.), and probably during the 60's or even 50's. This means that belief in the resurrection of Jesus was completely established less than 35 years after his time on Earth. Also, the Gospels were all transmitted orally for some time before being written down, which dates belief in the Resurrection back even further. The point of all this talk about dates is that there simply could not have been enough time for such radical myths about Jesus Christ to develop, which makes the Myth theory a highly implausible alternative to the actual Resurrection. Another problem with the Myth theory, which is much more significant than it might seem, is that the literary style is nothing like mythical stories of the time and culture in which the Gospels were written. C.S. Lewis, who was a renowned literary critic (and former atheist), wrote about this fact: "I have been reading poems, romances, vision-literature, legends, myths all my life. I know what they are like. I know that not one of [the Gospels] is like this" (Lewis). If the Gospels and other documents of the New Testament are not literal and accurate recordings of historical events, but merely fiction, then the authors were writing in a literary genre that didn't exist for at least another eighteen hundred years—realistic historical fiction. There are miracles recorded to be sure, but there are no frills, crazy events, or overly extravagant occurrences that one would expect to find in a myth. What we do find in these writings are countless, obscure, and ultimately unnecessary details that one would expect from an eyewitness account. An example of such a detail comes from the story of the woman caught in adultery, in which we are told that Jesus wrote on the ground with his finger (Jn 8:6, 8). That detail doesn't add anything substantial to the message of the story, so why was it included? Most likely, because it actually happened. This brings up another point that undermines the Myth theory. Several different authors of books and letters in the New Testament explicitly state that they are eyewitnesses to Jesus' life, death, and post-mortem appearances. Saint Luke opens his gospel in the following way:

> Inasmuch as many have undertaken to compile a narrative of the things which have been accomplished among us, just as they were delivered to us by those who from the beginning were eyewitnesses and ministers of the word, it seemed good to me also, having followed all things closely for some time past, to write an orderly account for you...that you may know the truth concerning the things of which you have been informed (Lk 1:1-4).

Saint Paul asserts in multiple letters that the Gospel he writes about is not a myth and that he is telling the literal truth:

> For I would have you know, brethren, that the gospel which was preached by me is not man's gospel. For I did not receive it from man, nor was I taught it, but it came through a revelation of Jesus Christ (Gal 1:11-12). I am speaking the truth in Christ, I am not lying; my conscience bears me witness in the Holy Spirit (Rom 9:1).

Saint Peter makes similar claims, written in his second letter, and spoken to the Jews in the book of Acts:

> For we did not follow cleverly devised myths when we made known to you the power and coming of our Lord Jesus Christ, but we were eyewitnesses of his majesty (2 Pet 1:16). "This Jesus God raised up, and of that we all are witnesses" (Acts 2:32).

Obviously, Saints Paul and Peter asserting that the Gospel is not a myth does not prove that it isn't one. However, if you were writing a mythical narrative and making claims about historical people and events that no one could check the truth or falsehood of, then why would you call attention to the possibility that the whole story could just be a myth? It would be like a drug dealer under investigation saying to the police officer, "There definitely isn't any cocaine inside the spare tire in the trunk." Inserting into a myth the possibility that the whole thing could just be a myth unnecessarily calls the credibility of the myth into question, and in doing so undermines its power to convince people. Also, if the authors of the New Testament claim it isn't myth, and it is, then they were lying, which takes us back to the problems of the Conspiracy theory.

The Inconvenient Truth

The resurrection of Jesus Christ from dead, while it is no small claim or easy proposition to accept, is the best explanation of all the historical data that we have. After Jesus died, why was his tomb found empty? Why did numerous people claim that Jesus appeared to them after his death? Why were all of the apostles and other followers of Jesus not afraid to die after their leader had just been brutally tortured and executed? Why does Christianity even exist? There is one possibility that answers all of these questions seamlessly and explains all the data we have: Because the resurrection of Jesus Christ from the dead is a real historical event in history. It *actually* happened. In itself, the Resurrection may not be a provable proposition. However, since all alternative attempts to explain the events following the death of Jesus fail miserably, it is completely reasonable to believe in the Resurrection. Once a year, we Christians get to participate in the glorious celebration of that day which literally changes everything, that transforms our existence from one of death and despair to one of life and hope—Easter. Let us pray:

Heavenly Father, give us the grace we need to experience the Resurrection of Your Son not as an abstract theological idea, a nice story, a myth, or theory to be discussed or enjoyed, but as a real, concrete, and historical fact that radically transforms everything in our lives. We ask this in the name of Jesus Christ our Lord, who defeated death that we might have life, Amen.

May God continue to bless you on your Lenten journey, and may you be renewed by a most blessed celebration of the Resurrection this Easter! Thanks for reading!

† Under the Mercy,

Chris Trummer

Sources:

Catholic Biblical Association (Great Britain). *The Holy Bible: Revised Standard Version, Catholic Edition*. New York: National Council of Churches of Christ in the USA, 1994. Print.

Lewis, Clive Staples. *Christian Reflections. Modern Theology and Biblical Criticism*. Ed Walter Hooper. Grand Rapids: William B. Eerdmans Publisher, 1967. Web.

Ratzinger, Joseph. *Jesus of Nazareth: Holy Week: From the Entrance into Jerusalem to the Resurrection*. San Francisco: Ignatius Press, 2011. Print.

Apathy: Spiritual Cancer

"Hell is not populated mainly by passionate rebels but by nice, bland, indifferent, respectable people who simply never gave a damn." – Peter Kreeft, *Christianity for Modern Pagans*

A couple of posts ago, I wrote about the concept of doubt, about what it is and the role it plays in the Christian life. In the 2008 film "Doubt," Philip Seymour Hoffman plays a priest named Father Flynn who gives a powerful homily about doubt. He goes so far as to claim that doubt can be as powerful of a motivator in life as certainty. That probably sounds far-fetched and even flaky. However, when considered more deeply, we observe that in ourselves and in others, the times in which we were driven most strongly into a deeper relationship with God were often those in which we had the least certainty. This is evident in human relationships as well. The people whom we find most agreeable and never argue with are usually the ones we are not as close to. Conversely, our closest friends tend to be the ones with whom we have experienced tension and even rough times with. The path to intimacy with and knowledge of any human being is marked by obstacles, and includes difficult terrain. However, whenever we make ourselves vulnerable, whenever we take a chance on another person, we are rarely disappointed. The first step on the path is believing that its end is worth reaching, that the destination is desirable. If you don't believe that true friendship is worth obtaining or even possible to obtain, then you won't be willing to put in the time and effort, and to endure the awkward and uncomfortable situations which are inevitable on the journey. There is a direct parallel to this in our relationship with God. Just as we can be indifferent or apathetic towards other people, we can feel the same way towards God and our faith. This is apathy, which is to the soul what cancer is to the body.

Love's Worst Enemy

"Indifference is more truly the opposite of love than hate is, for we can both love and hate the same person at the same time, but we cannot both

love and be indifferent to the same person at the same time." - Peter
Kreeft, *Prayer for Beginners*

To love is to care, but to hate also requires that you care—not necessarily
caring about what you're hating, but caring about something else and
experiencing the conflict between the two objects. For example, I can't
hate sin or vice unless I love goodness and virtue; I can't hate illness
unless I love health. If I don't first care about something, then it's
impossible to either love or hate it. If something or someone simply
doesn't matter to me, then it's not worth the energy of my love or my
hatred - it's irrelevant. What does this have to do with my relationship with
God? To put it plainly, a relationship with anyone, including God, begins
with taking interest in that person. Apathy is the absence of that interest.
In our culture today, there is a literal epidemic of apathy, especially
regarding religious questions. The number of people who actually hate
religion or God is extremely small. When faced with eternal questions
about God or the meaning of life, the overwhelming majority of non-
religious people do not respond with, "I reject that!" or, "No way!" but
simply, "I'm not interested." In other words, "...Meh." How is this
possible? How can a person be so existentially unconscious? It seems like
a spiritual disease, which is why I refer to apathy as "spiritual cancer." It is
like cancer in the way it begins as a small, relatively unnoticeable defect in
one area of a person's life and then slowly spreads to all the other areas,
and by the time the symptoms of it are noticed, it already has a deadly grip
on the person. In other ways, apathy is more like a virus, because unlike
cancer, it is infectious: it spreads from person to person rapidly. The
Catholic philosopher and scientist Blaise Pascal wrote about how bizarre
of a phenomenon apathy is in human beings:

> "Nothing is so important to man as his own state, nothing is so
> formidable to him as eternity; and thus it is not natural that there should
> be men indifferent to the loss of their existence, and to the perils of
> everlasting suffering. They are quite different with regard to all other
> things. They are afraid of mere trifles; they foresee them; they feel them.
> And this same man who spends so many days and nights in rage and
> despair for the loss of office, or for some imaginary insult to his honour,
> is the very one who knows without anxiety and without emotion that he

124

will lose all by death. It is a monstrous thing to see in the same heart and at the same time this sensibility to trifles and this strange insensibility to the greatest objects. It is an incomprehensible enchantment, and a supernatural slumber, which indicates as its cause an all-powerful force" (*Pensées*, #194).

Putting First Things First

We can all relate to being too sensible to "trifles." For example, isn't it strange that the same people who claim to be absolutely convicted in their belief in Christianity talk about the outcome of professional sports' games as if they actually mattered in any real and lasting sense? Every week, we declare, "I believe in the Resurrection of the body, and in life everlasting." Umm...What?! That's a radical and exciting concept! How can we really believe that and at the same time be distressed by the canceling of a TV show or attentive to the personal lives of celebrities? Pascal was right to call this condition an "incomprehensible enchantment," since it makes no logical sense whatsoever. As Kreeft wrote, "It's just as crazy not to be crazy about God as it is to be crazy about anything else" (Jesus Shock). This doesn't mean that there's nothing in this world worth taking interest in, or investing our time and effort into. Rather, it is simply the principle of "first things," of having our priorities straight. The first priority, based on the eternal nature of the question, has to be deciding whether or not we believe in God, and within that belief, how that affects our lives. In modern minds, there is a growing disconnect between the truth of an idea and the practical usefulness of it. C.S. Lewis cut to the heart of this thought pattern:

> Man is becoming as narrowly "practical" as the irrational animals. In lecturing to popular audiences I have repeatedly found it almost impossible to make them understand that I recommended Christianity because I thought it's affirmations to be objectively true. They are simply not interested in the question of truth or falsehood. They only want to know if it will be comforting, or "inspiring," or socially useful. Closely connected with this unhuman Practicality is indifference to, in contempt of, dogma. The popular point of view is unconsciously syncretistic; it is

widely believed that "all religions really mean the same thing" ("Modern Man and His Categories of Thought").

Do You Want the Bad News or the Good News?

If the guiding question in your investigation of God and religion is not "Is this true?" but "What can this do for me?" then what is being offered to you probably won't seem desirable. It is this self-centered approach that makes the work of evangelization and apologetics so difficult today. Convincing someone of the existence of God or the divinity of Jesus Christ is not an easy task, but harder still is the task of convincing them that such ideas matter in the first place. I've had more productive dialogue with atheists than with people who simply aren't interested in religious questions. It's easier to provide reasonable arguments than it is to instill passion. The reason why the Good News of Christianity doesn't sound good to many people is that they are unaware of the Bad News. Without recognizing and admitting our fallen nature, our brokenness, and our sin, we cannot recognize our need for a Savior. A savior saves you from something, as the words of that song say: "Amazing grace, how sweet the sound, that saved a wretch like me." Not a "good person," or even a "decent person," but a "wretch." Christ said, "Those who are well have no need of a physician, but those who are sick; I have not come to call the righteous, but sinners to repentance" (Lk 5:31-32). Once we see our sickness and wretchedness for what it is, we're immediately in the market for a physician, a savior.

Ignorance ≠ Bliss

Unfortunately, many people might be indifferent to God and religion because of some sort of "ignorance is bliss" mentality. This is dangerously presumptuous. An all-knowing God is perfectly capable of judging not only minds but hearts; not only beliefs but motivations and intentions: "I the LORD search the mind and try the heart, to give to every man according to his ways, according to the fruit of his doings" (Jer 17:10). Christ himself said, "For every one who asks receives, and he who seeks finds, and to him who knocks it will be opened" (Mt 7:8). This means that not asking, not seeking, and not knocking are not excusable. We often think that damnation consists only in hatred, cruelty, vengefulness, greed, and other more obvious vices. However, Christ seems to suggest that the primary determining factor in our salvation is not so much the level of moral perfection or virtue that we attain (we always could have done better), but whether or not we passionately seek God during our life. Pascal summarized this succinctly in the *Pensées*:

> There are only three types of people; those who have found God and serve him; those who have not found God and seek him, and those who live not seeking, or finding him. The first are rational and happy; the second rational and unhappy; and the third foolish and unhappy (Pensées, #257).

Don't Be Content With (A)pathetic Life!

Notice that there is no fourth group consisting of people who find God without seeking him, because that is impossible. Apathy is toxic to faith, and to any rational human endeavor for that matter. It reduces the glory of human nature, which is naturally truth seeking, to a pathetic, animalistic, pleasure-addicted existence. The chemotherapy or radiation for the cancer of apathy is nothing less than a personal encounter with Jesus Christ. This encounter can happen in a variety of ways, but it is most powerful and most tangible in the Sacraments of the Church, and especially in the Eucharist. Consuming the Eucharist is like chemotherapy; adoring the Eucharist is like radiation. That being said, don't have a "wait and see" attitude about your spiritual life and relationship with God—get to the Doctor! May the Lord bless us, protect us from all evil, and bring us to everlasting life, Amen.

† Under the Mercy,

Chris Trummer

Sources:

Catholic Biblical Association (Great Britain). *The Holy Bible: Revised Standard Version, Catholic Edition.* New York: National Council of Churches of Christ in the USA, 1994. Print.

Kreeft, Peter. *Christianity for Modern Pagans.* Ignatius Press, 1993.
    " . *Prayer for Beginners.* Ignatius Press, 2000.
    " . *Jesus Shock.* St. Augustines Press, 2008.

Lewis, Clive Staples. *Present Concerns: Essays.* "Modern Man and His Categories of Thought." 1946, p. 65.

Pascal, Blaise. *Pensées.* E.P. Duton & Co., Inc., 1958.

Redefining Marriage: Why Rainbows and Hashtags Don't Change Reality

Rainbows and Hashtags

Since June 26th, many Americans have been joyfully celebrating, while others have been troubled, saddened, and even angry. Social media has exploded with comments from both supporters and opponents of same-sex marriage, and many profile pictures are now sporting rainbow backgrounds. On the front lines of Twitter, the hashtag #lovewins is trending. I am speaking, of course, about the recent Supreme Court decision in the Obergefell v. Hodges case which ruled that all state bans against same-sex marriage were unconstitutional. I refer to the Supreme Court's decision as the "redefinition of marriage" and not "marriage equality" because I do not believe the court's ruling achieved, nor that any court ruling can ever achieve, actual equality between the marriages of same-sex couples and that of opposite-sex couples. This post is an attempt to explain why that is the case. Also, while the recent Supreme Court decision is certainly significant, I realize that it is only a visible mile marker on a road that we as a country have been traveling on for a while now (36 states already recognized same-sex marriage prior to the Supreme Court's ruling). In fact, marriage in this country has been under the process of redefinition for the better part of a century now. The most recent decision is not a cause, but an effect, not the underlying illness, but a symptom, of a confused and mistaken understanding of human sexuality and civilization. The Supreme Court's decision is not some shocking new development, but the logical conclusion of the redefinition of marriage that has already been taking place. However, if we look to the more recent past, it's difficult to understand how we got here from where we were. Just twenty years ago, both major political parties in the United States were (at least formally) opposed to same-sex marriage. Also, according to Gallup polls, from March 1996 to May 2015, the percentage of Americans opposed to same-sex marriage went from 68% to 37% (Gallup). Today, if you disagree with same-sex marriage, you are usually labeled intolerant, hateful, discriminative, and/or bigoted, and the way things are going in this country, you will soon be silenced as if you were a member of some racist group like the KKK. How did this happen? How did five un-elected judges redefine marriage in a democratic society that until recently embraced the millennia-old definition? Well, just as "Rome wasn't built in a day," Rome didn't fall in a day either.

The (Really) Old Definition of Marriage

In order to understand how marriage is being redefined, it is necessary to first understand what the original definition was. A working definition of the traditional view of marriage could be: "The civil and legal institution consisting of one man and one woman, for the purpose of ensuring their fidelity and accountability to one another and any children they might create." You probably noticed that this definition does not include the word "love." Isn't that a mistake? No, because even though love is understood by most modern cultures as a necessary prerequisite for marriage, and even though it may be the best psychological and spiritual cement to hold a marriage together, it is not quantitative or measurable in any legal sense and therefore should not hold any interest of the state. If the state is interested in recognizing marriages because of love, then it should be interested in recognizing friendships because of loyalty, shared interests, etc.. Last time I checked, the state isn't issuing friendship licenses (but I'm sure there's a movement for that too). It's important to understand that the historical exclusion of same-sex couples from the institution of marriage was due to the definition of marriage, and its understood purpose in a society, not intolerance, hatred, bigotry, or any other discriminative beliefs, even if these have unfortunately existed to varying degrees in many cultures throughout history. That is why cultures that were at once completely accepting of homosexual behavior and relationships, such as ancient Greece and Rome, were at the same time opposed to the idea of same-sex marriage. Dismissing all arguments against same-sex marriage as religion or fear-based discrimination is not only intellectual laziness or cowardice, but historically false.

How Did We Get Here?

Understanding the traditional definition of marriage, let us now examine the factors that led to the Supreme Court decision late last month. The traditional definition of marriage includes and assumes the marital act—sexual intercourse. Sexual intercourse has a two-fold purpose by nature: the unitive (it brings the couple closer together), and the pro-creative (it creates new life).* Before sex could be separated from marriage, pro-creation had to be separated from sex, which leads to the first major factor in the redefinition of marriage, contraception (birth control). The second major factor was the elimination of the permanence of marriage, which we will discuss shortly.

* This is not merely an opinion or religious belief—secular biology and psychology textbooks will provide you with the same conclusion.

Out-of-Control Birth Control

Contraception was the first major chink in the armor of traditional marriage. How is this so? The popular view on contraception began to shift dramatically when the Church of England decided that contraception was morally permissible within the context of marriage at the Lambeth Conference in 1930, and nearly all other denominations followed suit. Prior to that decision in 1930, every major Christian denomination was opposed to contraception. Today, the Catholic Church (along with most of the Orthodox Churches) is more or less the only remaining opposition to contraception. However, while the teaching of Catholic Church against contraception is quite clear, most Catholics in modern countries do not subscribe to this doctrine, and most surveys indicate that Catholic married couples use contraception just as much as anyone else. So, what does contraception have to do with marriage? A great deal, actually. The traditional understanding of marriage is that it serves as the foundation for a family, and that healthy marriages are open to children. In other words, marriage includes the marital act (sexual intercourse), and under normal circumstances, that act eventually produces children. Contraception blocks the natural pro-creative mechanisms by various means and effectively eliminates the pro-creative element of sexual intercourse. The removal of the pro-creative element has completely transformed the way that people view sexual intercourse and relationships. Before contraception was widely accepted and available, there was a huge implication of commitment when a person decided to have sexual relations with another person. This level of commitment is both welcomed and well-grounded within the context of a healthy marriage. Outside of marriage, however, pregnancy is usually an unwelcome and even frightening reality, especially for the woman if she is not financially independent. Contraception changed all of this, and by separating pro-creation from sexual intercourse, produced in people an entirely new attitude towards the commitment involved in relationships and marriages. This new attitude, along with other cultural and social influences at the time, produced the so-called "sexual revolution" of the 1960s. It is safe to say that contraception opened the door for marriage to no longer necessitate, or at least imply, the creation and raising of children. Abortion, which is nothing more than back-up birth control, severed whatever pro-creative threads remained in the marriage equation, and children became a commodity or lifestyle "choice" for married couples, instead of a gift and blessing that naturally proceeded from their union.

Until Death or "Irreconcilable Differences" Do Us Part

The traditional definition of marriage also includes the element of permanence or endurance (you know, the whole, "till death do us part" bit). This element also died, at least in the legal sense, with the advent of "no-fault" divorce. In 1969, California was the first state to adopt a no-fault divorce law, which allowed a couple to be granted a divorce without requiring either party to provide evidence of a breech in the marriage contract (e.g., an affair, abuse, etc.). The divorce rate then began to rise rapidly. In the 1950s, the percentage of marriages that ended in divorce was less than 10%, and by the early 1980s, that rate peaked at just over 50%. The divorce rate has since been slowly declining, but it remains relatively high, and that is probably at least in part due to the decreased marriage rate (most of people getting married now are the ones who are more serious about it). Removing permanence from the definition of marriage contributed to a less-serious view of the institution, and coupled with the removal of the pro-creative element, reduced the perceived commitment involved in marriage to an all-time low.

The New (But Not Improved) Definition of Marriage

We've considered what has been eliminated from the traditional definition of marriage. The new definition of marriage does not necessitate an openness to life, or even sexual activity for that matter, and does not necessitate a life-long commitment. The question naturally rises: What's left? What is the new definition of marriage in this country? Chief Justice Anthony Kennedy, majority leader in the Supreme Court decision, stated the following:

> No union is more profound than marriage, for it embodies the highest ideals of love, fidelity, devotion, sacrifice, and family. In forming a marital union, two people become something greater than once they were. As some of the petitioners in these cases demonstrate, marriage embodies a love that may endure even past death. It would misunderstand these men and women to say they disrespect the idea of marriage. Their plea is that they do respect it, respect it so deeply that they seek to find its fulfillment for themselves. Their hope is not to be condemned to live in loneliness, excluded from one of civilization's oldest institutions. They ask for equal dignity in the eyes of the law. The Constitution grants them that right. The judgment of the Court of Appeals for the Sixth Circuit is reversed. It is so ordered (Obergefell v. Hodges).

What is the new definition of marriage based on then? Love. Chris, what's wrong with that? Don't you want people who love each other to have the same rights as everyone else? Shouldn't "love win," as the hashtag says? Let's be clear. There is absolutelynothing wrong with the definition of marriage being based on love. However, is that all there is to marriage? If so, then marriage seems strikingly similar to every other healthy human relationship. Heck, Jesus even told us to love our enemies (Mt 5:44). If love is the sole prerequisite for marriage, then what does the new definition of marriage logically include? First of all, it certainly includes polygamous marriages (marriages involving three or more people). If you question whether or not there's a demand for polygamous marriage, consider hit shows like TLC's "Sister Wives" and HBO's "Big Love," along with recent statements from polygamist activists in the wake of the Obergefell v. Hodges decision. In fact, Chief Justice John Roberts, one of the four dissenting judges, commented on this exact implication:

> "It is striking how much of the majority's reasoning would apply with equal force to the claim of a fundamental right to plural marriage. If "[t]here is dignity in the bond between two men or two women who seek to marry and in their autonomy to make such profound choices," ... why would there be any less dignity in the bond between three people who, in exercising their autonomy, seek to make the profound choice to marry?"

Second, the new definition logically includes incestuous marriages (marriages between siblings, parent-child marriages, etc.). You might be surprised to hear that incestuous marriages are already technically legal in New Jersey. Also, a recent New York magazine article tells the story of an 18 year old girl who wants to move to New Jersey to marry her long-estranged biological father. If a person is logically consistent in his or her application of #lovewins, then this shouldn't be alarming or disturbing at all. I can already here the question: "Who are you to tell two people they don't love each other?" Once you base a civil institution entirely on a subjective feeling, you've abandoned any logical basis from which to exclude anyone from that institution. Defining something always involves saying that the thing is this, and not that—some things are always excluded. Now, with the new definition, what is marriage not?

Reality is Harder to Redefine Than Words

Supporters of the redefinition of marriage would like to believe that decisions likeObergefell v. Hodges constitute an expansion in the institution of marriage. This is only true if marriage is merely a personal freedom like the freedom of speech, to be fought for and universally granted, rather than a civil institution that arises naturally from human nature, both biologically and socially. The battle cry, "Marriage equality!" reveals that the new definition is of the former. However, a little clear thinking reveals why there will never be an actual "equality" between homosexual so-called "marriages" and heterosexual marriages—they are fundamentally different. Heterosexual marriages satisfy the natural complementarity between the male and female sexes, and are ordered toward the creation of new life, while homosexual "marriages" are not complementary and are not ordered towards new life. Heterosexual marriage is a self-sufficient institution—homosexual "marriage" is not, because behind every homosexual couple there are two heterosexual couples. In other words, homosexual "marriage" needs heterosexuality, but heterosexual marriage does not need homosexuality.

Why Does the Government Care About Marriage?

Redefining marriage to include relationships such as two people of the same gender is simply a watering down of the definition of the word "marriage." It's the equivalent of saying that a dog and a cat are the same animal by reducing the definition of each to, "A four-legged mammal commonly owned as a pet by human beings." In an analogous way, it can only be accurate to call the relationship between same-sex couples a marriage if by the word "marriage" one simply means, "a state-issued certificate of approval on the romantic relationship between two persons." If, on the other hand, by "marriage" one is referring to something that is in any way similar to the millennia-old definition, then calling same-sex unions "marriages" is meaningless. After all, if marriage is nothing more than a "certificate of love," then why is the state interested in marriage in the first place? The only reasons for the state to be interested in marriage are 1) To keep both parties in a couple accountable to each other, which prevents abuse and neglect (one person can't just walk out on the other), and 2) To keep couples accountable to any children they may produce or adopt. Every child has two biological parents: a mother and a father. Marriage is the social and legal cement that binds together mother, father, and children. There's no other legitimate reason for the state to be involved in the marriage business (the key word there is: legitimate).

But Wait, Weren't They "Born That Way?"

Supporters of same-sex marriage often assert that people who experience same-sex attraction (SSA) were "born that way." Before even attempting to explain exactly how a person comes to have SSA, it's worth asking: Even if people were born with these attractions, would that be a sufficient reason for the state to recognize the union of two men or two women as a marriage? No, because of the reasons mentioned above. It's not in the state's interest to determine whose romantic relationships are valid and whose are not—it's only in the state's interest to guarantee people their Constitutional rights, protect them from abuse, and hold them accountable to the people whom they are legally responsible for (i.e., spouses and children). With that being said, there is literally NO scientific evidence to support the idea that people with SSA are "born that way." Eight extensive studies have recently been conducted on SSA using thousands of identical twins. Identical twins share the exact same DNA, as well as the same pre-natal environments. In other words, when it comes to anything that is genetically determined (e.g., hair color, height, bone structure, etc.) identical twins share a one-to-one concordance (correlation). So, is there a one-to-one concordance for identical twins when it comes to having SSA? No. In fact, in all the studies of identical twins, the concordance found for SSA was around 11-14%. That means that when one twin identified as homosexual, there was an 11-14% chance that the other twin did. Scientifically speaking, this is a complete disproof of the "born that way" theory. New Zealand geneticist Dr. Neal Whitehead, author of *My Genes Made Me Do It! A Scientific Look at Sexual Orientation*, concluded the following about the genetic basis for homosexuality:

> One thing seems clear: any genetic contribution to SSA is much less than in most traits for which genetic influence has been measured. SSA seems 90% a result of random factors. SSA is in fact a good example of not being "born that way"! . . . Saying a trait is, e.g., 10% "genetic" is nothing extraordinary. There is at least a 10% genetic effect in anything humans are and do, simply because without bodies we can't act in the environment at all. "Genetic" effects are experienced by everyone because we all have bodies. So homosexuality is like any other human trait. Any genetic effects are mostly quite indirect, and for

SSA they are weak. Also, they become relatively less important in the face of contrary environmental input (Whitehead 175).

How Should Christians Respond?

As the implications of the legal redefinition of marriage play themselves out, it will become more necessary for the Church to speak the truth about human sexuality and marriage with a united and clear voice. Not to sound pessimistic, but you can expect to see more problems with theological dissent amongst lay faithful and clergy alike regarding this issue and related issues. Also, there will be an increase in legal battles against the Catholic Church and organizations affiliated with the Church. People will sue over disagreements about the content of Catholic primary and secondary school curricula regarding human sexuality and the institution of marriage. The good news is, in the Catholic Church, we do pretty well under persecution. In fact, every period of major growth in the Church, quantitative and qualitative, was the direct result of endured persecution. That's the problem with "those pesky Christians"—the easiest way for us to know if were doing the will of God is whether or not we're being persecuted. To the lay faithful who are troubled and concerned, Christ speaks the following words: "If the world hates you, know that it has hated me before it hated you. If you were of the world, the world would love its own; but because you are not of the world, but I chose you out of the world, therefore the world hates you" (John 15:18-20). And to our shepherds, to all the bishops, priests, and deacons in whom we trust to guide us, Saint Paul wrote the following:

> I charge you in the presence of God and of Christ Jesus who is to judge the living and the dead, and by his appearing and his kingdom: preach the word, be urgent in season and out of season, convince, rebuke, and exhort, be unfailing in patience and in teaching. For the time is coming when people will not endure sound teaching, but having itching ears they will accumulate for themselves teachers to suit their own likings, and will turn away from listening to the truth and wander into myths. As for you, always be steady, endure suffering, do the work of an evangelist, fulfill your ministry (2 Tim 4:1-5).

As Christians, it's not just preferable that we know how to explain the truth to people—it's our duty (see Mt. 28:18-20). Even in the midst of widespread cultural and legal confusion, we have the certainty of belonging to the Church, which is the "pillar and foundation of the truth" (1 Tim 3:15). The Church has survived the rise and fall of many empires, and the moral decline of the United States of America will not be an exception to that.

> For though we live in the world we are not carrying on a worldly war, for the weapons of our warfare are not worldly but have divine power to destroy strongholds. We destroy arguments and every proud obstacle to the knowledge of God, and take every thought captive to obey Christ" (2 Cor 10:3-5).

What Would Jesus Do?

Many supporters of same-sex marriage will go so far as to say that Jesus would be in favor of it. It's true that Jesus never condemned anyone. It's true that Jesus accepted people who everyone else hated and cast out. It's true that Jesus wasn't afraid to challenge peoples' understanding of human nature and upset the cultural norms of his time. However, Jesus never pretended that sin was not sin, or that what we do with our bodies doesn't really matter so long as we love each other. To the woman caught in adultery, he said, "Neither do I condemn you; go, and do not sin again" (Jn 8:11, emphasis added). Jesus was a committed Jew who said: "Think not that I have come to abolish the law and the prophets; I have come not to abolish them but to fulfill them" (Mt 5:17). To say that, because we have no record of Jesus explicitly condemning homosexual behavior or same-sex marriage, that those things are therefore morally permissible or even praiseworthy, is an extremely narrow and confused view of Divine Revelation at best, and a dishonest hijacking of Sacred Scripture for one's personal agenda at worst. It's ridiculous to think that something as foundational as marriage was equivalent in the Mosaic Law to something like a hand-washing ritual. You can depart from the truth if you choose, but you can't bring the Truth

Incarnate down with you. He's bigger than your agenda, and more trendy than your hashtags. #truthwins

God bless you and thanks for reading!

† Under the Mercy,

Chris Trummer

Sources:

Catholic Biblical Association (Great Britain). *The Holy Bible: Revised Standard Version, Catholic Edition*. New York: National Council of Churches of Christ in the USA, 1994. Print.

Gallup. "Marriage."
URL: http://www.gallup.com/poll/117328/marriage.aspx. Retrieved on 07-07-2015. Web.

Supreme Court of the United States. *Oberfell v. Hodges*. URL: .
Retrieved on 07-http://www.supremecourt.gov/opinions/14pdf/14-556_3204.pdf 07-2015. Web.

Whitehead, Neal E.. "My Genes Made Me Do It! A Scientific Look at Sexual Orientation". 3rd Ed. Huntington House Pub, 1999.

The Gospel According to Me: Why the Bible Alone Isn't Enough

> "If you believe what you like in the gospels, and reject what you don't like, it is not the gospel you believe, but yourself." - Saint Augustine

One of the most destructive beliefs among modern Christians, which has its origin primarily in the Protestant Reformation, is the doctrine known as "sola scriptura"(literally, "scripture alone"). Sola scriptura is the belief that the documents of the Bible are all that is necessary for a complete and proper understanding of the Christian faith, as revealed in the person of Jesus Christ. The Catholic understanding of Divine Revelation is that such an understanding also requires Sacred Tradition—all of the teachings lived and taught by the Church throughout history, which are not explicitly found in the texts of scripture—as well as the Magisterium, which is the teaching office of the Church. Today, most Christians (and probably most Catholics included) tend to downplay or even outright reject any teaching authority or source of Christian doctrine that is external to the Bible itself. Many such people refer to themselves as "Bible Christians," and take pride in their claim not to follow any so-called "traditions of men." There are serious problems with this growing breed of Christianity: 1) it's not Biblical, 2) it's not historical, and 3) it's not logical.

"Where is THAT in the Bible?"

The most common objection I encounter to any given teaching of the Catholic Church is that it isn't found in the Bible. "Where is the Pope in the Bible?" "Where in the Bible does it say that I have to confess my sins to a priest?" "Where in the Bible does it say that Mary was conceived without sin?" "Where do you find purgatory in the Bible?" And the list goes on and on. The truth is, most of these teachings do in fact have a strong Biblical foundation, even if they are not explicit (the word "Trinity" isn't found in the Bible either). However, before offering any evidence from scripture to counter the claims against any particular teaching, the best question for the Catholic to ask is, "Why do I have to prove every Catholic doctrine or teaching from the Bible?" In demanding that every teaching be explicitly stated in the Bible, the non-Catholic person is assuming the truth of sola scriptura. This assumption is not only unwarranted, but ironically is itself unbiblical. Sola scriptura is self-referentially incoherent, that is, it disproves itself. Where in the Bible does it say that all the truths of the Christian faith are found in the Bible? It doesn't. On the contrary, there are many references in the Bible to the need for authority and tradition. For example, John concludes his gospel account with the words, "But there are also many other things which Jesus did; were every one of them to be written, I suppose that the world itself could not contain the books that would be written (Jn 21:25). Saint Paul too alludes to the importance of the unwritten, orally transmitted teachings of the Church numerous times in different epistles:

> I commend you because you remember me in everything and maintain the traditions even as I have delivered them to you (1 Cor 11:2). So then, brethren, stand firm and hold to the traditions which you were taught by us, either by word of mouth or by letter (2 Thes 2:15).

> Now we command you, brethren, in the name of our Lord Jesus Christ, that you keep away from any brother who is living in idleness and not in accord with the tradition that you received from us (2 Thes 3:6).

> You then, my son, be strong in the grace that is in Christ Jesus, and what you have heard from me before many witnesses entrust to faithful men who will be able to teach others also (2 Tim 2:1-2).

The most common Bible verses cited in favor of sola scriptura are John 20:31 and 2 Timothy 3:16-17. John 20:31 reads, "[T]hese are written that you may believe that Jesus is the Christ, the Son of God, and that believing you may have life in his name." This verse at most claims that John's gospel account contains sufficient information for a person to believe that Jesus is the Christ, the Messiah. It in no way claims that the rest of the Bible (which hadn't even been compiled yet) is all that one needs for salvation, or even for doing Christian theology for that matter. The verses from 2 Timothy read:

> "All Scripture is inspired by God and profitable for teaching, for reproof, for correction, and for training in righteousness, that the man of God may be complete, equipped for every good work" (2 Tim 3:16-17).

All Saint Paul is saying here is that Sacred Scripture is useful for many things. Saying that Scripture can make Christians "complete" and "equipped for every good work" doesn't mean that it is completely sufficient for understanding and living the Christian faith. To understand this, imagine a soldier equipped with the most state-of-the-art weaponry, armor, and other high-tech tactical gear, while at the same time having no training, guidance, or leadership for the use and employment of that weaponry and gear. Needless to say, he or she would in no sense be "sufficient" as a soldier. Making this important distinction requires that one understand the difference between *formal* sufficiency and *material* sufficiency. Like all the combined equipment of the soldier, the Word of God in Sacred Scripture is materially sufficient. In other words, if you have the complete Bible then you have all the raw data you need. However, there is an enormous gap between having all the necessary data and having the correct interpretation of that data.

Another fact that undermines a sola scriptura interpretation of Saint Paul's words here was well articulated by Blessed John Henry Cardinal Newman (a convert from Anglicanism), who wrote:

> Now, a good part of the New Testament was not written in his [Timothy's] boyhood: Some of the Catholic [universal] epistles were not written even when Paul wrote this, and none of the books of the New Testament were then placed on the canon of the Scripture books. He refers, then, to the scriptures of the Old Testament, and, if the argument from this passage proved anything, it would prove too much, viz., that the scriptures of the New Testament were not necessary for a rule of faith.

Inspired Table of Contents?

Speaking of the canon of Scripture (the list designating which books belong in the Bible), where is this found in the Bible? Where in the Bible does it say which books should be in the Bible? It doesn't. The canon of

Scripture is in fact part of the Tradition of the Catholic Church, and any person who believes and trusts in the Bible also trusts, consciously or unconsciously, in the authority of the Catholic Church to compile and maintain the Bible with all of its contents down through the centuries to the present day (or at least until the 16th century). There were literally hundreds of different documents in circulation during the early centuries of Christianity, and yet the New Testament contains only 27 of them. Many of the documents exclude from the official canon are regarded to this day as historically, theologically, and spiritually valuable. The question is: Why didn't they "make the cut?" The short answer is, because the bishops and pope of the Catholic Church collectively decided that, regardless of whatever value those books and letters did or still do have, they were not inspired by God. Have you ever wondered why there are just the four gospels (Matthew, Mark, Luke, and John)? There are also the gospels of Peter, Judas, Thomas, Mary Magdalene, etc.. The reason is, apart from having sketchy historical origins, these claimed gospels contained teachings and events which contradict what is known as the "deposit of faith," the collected oral, written, and practiced teachings handed down from the apostles to the bishops of the time. This is the same reasoning that excludes later alleged revelations and inspired texts, such as the Qur'an and the Book of Mormon. These contradict what was already revealed by Jesus Christ to the apostles and handed down to the Church in every age. Without the existence of the Catholic Church from the time of the apostles, and her constant protection and teaching of the Bible, any claims about the Bible's authenticity, accuracy, and Divine inspiration are unfounded. That is why Saint Augustine wrote the following:

> Should you meet with a person not yet believing the gospel, how would you reply to him were he to say, "I do not believe?" For my part, I should not believe the gospel except as moved by the authority of the Catholic Church ("Against the Epistle of Manichæus Called Fundamental").

Christ told the apostles, "Behold, I am with you always, to the close of the age" (Mt 28:20, emphasis added). Not "for a few hundred years," or "once the Bible is written," or "when authentic Christianity returns 1500 years from now," but "always, to the close of the age."

The Implications of Sola Scriptura

The doctrine of sola scriptura is logically inconsistent with the teaching of Jesus Christ, who himself prayed:

> "I do not pray for these only, but also for those who believe in me through their word, that they may all be one; even as you, Father, are in me, and I in you, that they also may be in us, so that the world may believe that you have sent me. (Jn 17:20-21).

Believing in the "Bible alone," or in a purely subjective version of Christianity that is about "Jesus and me," is not only harmful to one's own spiritual health, but also greatly undermines the credibility of the message of Christianity to the rest of the world. When non-Christians see the tens of thousands of different interpretations of Christianity in the world today, how can we blame them for doubting the possibility of ever finding the true church, or for thinking that it's all merely man-made? Instead of seeing a strong, clear, and united witness of the Good News, they see what looks like a complicated spider web of conflicting and contradicting traditions, doctrines, and practices. This makes Christianity look like a private, do-it-yourself project instead of the Body of Christ, the "light of the world," the "city set on a hill" that cannot be hidden (Mt 5:14). A typically modern view of the Body of Christ, that is, of the Church, is that it is an invisible, purely spiritual reality with no concrete human institution, structure, hierarchy, or organization. What this view ultimately translates to is an illusion of unity among Christians, with the reality being widespread division, rampant relativism, and a complete distortion of the true Christian faith. Again, this is a tragedy not only for the many Christians who are led away from the truth themselves, but also for the unbelievers who are deprived of the opportunity to experience that truth in a way that is complete, consistent, and compelling. It is a beautiful gift to believe that the Bible is the Word of God, that it is inspired by Him and therefore infallible (without error) as a source of truth. However, an infallible textbook without an infallible teacher is open to every conceivable misinterpretation. If you've ever had Jehovah's Witnesses or Mormons come to your door, then you've experienced this firsthand.

Saint Peter himself warned the early Christians about private interpretation, in this case regarding the letters of Paul:

> [O]ur beloved brother Paul wrote to you according to the wisdom given him, speaking of this as he does in all his letters. There are some things in them hard to understand, which the ignorant and unstable twist to their own destruction, as they do the other Scriptures. You therefore, beloved, knowing this beforehand, beware lest you be carried away with the error of lawless men and lose your own stability (2 Pet 3:15-17).

The Humility to Be Led

The relativism that plagues our culture is becoming more and more of a problem within Christianity itself. When a person becomes convinced that finding the truth is impossible, they are naturally led to despair—to despair about God and, consequently, to abandon any hope that one's life has any objective meaning. The idea that we can assign our own meaning to our lives, that we can be "free" from the "oppression" of dogmas, creeds, and all other authority, is initially exciting and seemingly liberating. However, there is an overflowing library of human experience that disproves this philosophy, and reveals it to be empty, unfulfilling, and unworthy of our human nature, which longs for so much more. Jesus Christ never wrote anything, nor is there any evidence that he commanded his disciples to write anything. He did, however, tell them to, "...make disciples of all nations, baptizing them in the name of the Father and of the Son and of the Holy Spirit, teaching them to observe all that I have commanded you" (Mt 28:19-20). In their wisdom and under the guidance of the Holy Spirit, the apostles and other Christians did eventually decide to write down the message of the gospel. The Bible thus belongs to the Church and in the Church, not for her to wield as an instrument of power or manipulation, but for her to serve and safeguard as God's living and active Word spoken to His children. The role of all Christians is to be steeped in Scripture, to read it, study it, pray it, and live it. However, we do all of this in a way that does not contradict, but rather conforms to, the constant teaching of the Church handed down and developed since the time of the apostles. To do this requires the humility to be led, to relinquish total control over your life, having hands that are open to receive the gifts God wants to give us through His Church.

Who is Your Final Authority?

When it comes to understanding Sacred Scripture, everyone has some final authority for interpretation. The question is: Who is that authority for you? Is it yourself? Are you following the true gospel or "The Gospel According to Me?" Many people claim that the Holy Spirit guides their reading and interpreting of the Bible. It's true that the Holy Spirit is active in the lives of all baptized Christians, and Christians of every tradition and creed prove that everyday by the way they live their lives and seek to follow Christ. However, Christ promised that after his Ascension, he would send us the Holy Spirit to guide us into all truth (Jn 16:13). The Holy Spirit does not guide Christians into the "truth" of over 30,000 denominations —that would be a contradiction—for He is the Spirit of unity, and "God is not a God of confusion but of peace" (1 Cor 14:33). If you're a Christian and you find yourself subscribing to doctrines or practices that were not taught or lived by any Christians for the first 1500 or more years of Christianity (except perhaps a few condemned heretics), then it's time to reconsider why you believe those things. I'll close now with the words of Saint Paul:

> I appeal to you, brethren, by the name of our Lord Jesus Christ, that all of you agree and that there be no dissensions among you, but that you be united in the same mind and the same judgment. . . . Is Christ divided? (1 Cor 1:10,13)

Christ is of course *not* divided, and just as he promised, he has not left us orphans (Jn 14:18), but instead placed us gently in the arms of Mother Church, against whom the gates of hell shall not prevail (Mt 16:18). Let us all continue to pray for the unity of all Christians, in response to Christ's prayer that we "may all be one." Thank you for reading—God bless!

† Under the Mercy,
Chris Trummer

The Allegory of the Marathon

Many of you may be familiar with the Allegory of the Cave created by the Ancient Greek philosopher Plato. For those who aren't, Plato's allegory likens the work of a philosopher to that of a man who frees prisoners from a Cave, in which they have been imprisoned their entire lives. The prisoners' view of reality is completely distorted by their captors, who force them to look only at a wall, on which they cast shadows using various costumes and props. Once released from the Cave, the prisoners finally experience reality as it really is, by seeing actual objects in the light of the sun, instead of mere shadows by the dim light of a fire. To Plato, the work of a philosopher was one of liberation, which is why his Cave allegory is so fitting and so famous.

I would now like to offer a different allegory: the Allegory of the Marathon. During and after the experience of my first marathon in Springfield, Illinois last weekend, I realized that there are some striking parallels between running a marathon and the Christian spiritual life. Some of these parallels are more obvious, and others more subtle. I do not claim to have any original theological insights or concepts to offer. Rather, I simply thought my recent experience could perhaps shed some light on certain aspects of Christianity, instead of only burning a few thousand calories and leaving my legs really, really, sore . . . really.

A marathon is a 26.2 mile foot race. Most marathon training plans have you begin 18 weeks prior to the race (assuming that you already able to run at least 4 miles without walking). For most runners, the race itself takes them over 4 hours—it took me 4 hours, 24 minutes, and 57 seconds, which is a relatively modest pace of just over 10 minutes per mile, and just shy of my goal of 10 minutes/mile flat. Obviously, running a marathon seems either too difficult or not worthwhile to most people, evidenced by the fact that only about 0.5% of the U.S. population has ever completed one. Apart from simply being difficult, there are several other deeper parallels between marathon running and Christianity that I will now attempt to relate.

> Therefore, since we are surrounded by so great a cloud of witnesses, let us also lay aside every weight, and sin which clings so closely, and let us run with perseverance the race that is set before us (Heb 12:1).

When the author of the letter to the Hebrews writes "cloud of witnesses," he's referring to those who have gone before us and excelled in the faith, those who lived lives of heroic charity, as well as those who gave the ultimate witness to the faith in martyrdom. This is the communion of saints, who not only inspire and motivate us by the example of their holy lives, but who also constantly intercede for us in the presence of God by their prayers. In an similar way, there are almost always people who inspire and motivate us to run a marathon. When we see other people like ourselves accomplishing something difficult or reaching some goal, it is easier for us to visualize ourselves achieving those same things. Personally, while I've been a fan of distance running for several years, I definitely wouldn't have considered running the marathon in Springfield this year if it weren't for the example and encouragement of my bishop, Bishop Thomas John Paprocki. Last weekend's marathon was his 21st marathon in 21 years. His dedication to and love for running, especially for it's contribution to his spiritual life, is very inspiring to me.

Counting the Cost

> "For which of you, desiring to build a tower, does not first sit down and count the cost, whether he has enough to complete it? Otherwise, when he has laid a foundation, and is not able to finish, all who see it begin to mock him, saying, 'This man began to build, and was not able to finish.'" (Lk 14:28-30).

Jesus tells us that if we want to be his disciples, we must first "count the cost" and understand just how much following him is going to require of us (SPOILER ALERT: It's literally everything). While a marathon does not ask "everything" of us the way Jesus does, it does require a great deal of commitment, discipline, and fortitude. Both becoming a faithful disciple of Christ and a marathon finisher involve taking the task seriously—you cannot become either of them by accident or by half-heartedly drifting into them. It takes a conscious and deliberate choice, followed by a continued commitment. There will be days when you don't feel like going to Mass, or praying, or reading your Bible. Likewise, there are training days when you don't feel like skipping a fun social activity to run 10 miles. However, in both cases you have to remember your commitment, and that you're not "in it" simply for a feeling, but for something far deeper and more enduring, even if you can't fully understand that something yet. Remaining faithful to your training, whether in the faith or in running, is the key to bearing fruit when the time comes to actually "run the race."

Training for Body and Soul

> Every athlete exercises self-control in all things. They do it to receive a perishable wreath, but we an imperishable. Well, I do not run aimlessly, I do not box as one beating the air; but I pommel my body and subdue it, lest after preaching to others I myself should be disqualified (1 Cor 9:25-27).

Many people, when they see someone displaying some impressive skill or achieving a praiseworthy goal, will say something along the lines of, "Well, I could do that too if I practiced/trained x hours a day." The problem with this attitude is that practicing or training is an essential part of doing anything well—not some handicap needed by a less-talented minority. We don't praise the skill of an accomplished violinist because we're under the false impression that he or she never had to practice the instrument. Rather, we marvel even more at the person's skill because of all the practice we imagine it must have taken to acquire. To offer a faith-related example: We don't admire Mother Teresa because being holy and living a heroic life of service to the poorest of the poor in Calcutta was easy for her—we do so because that was extraordinarily difficult for her at times! The training needed for both a healthy body and a healthy soul isn't some unique and separate set of exercises. It simply involves starting to do the thing you want to do well, and starting to act like the person you want to be. You can start training for a marathon by running one mile, and you can start becoming a saint by doing one seemingly insignificant act of kindness. After all, "He who is faithful in a very little is faithful also in much" (Lk 16:10).

The Purification of Motivation

[F]or a little while you may have to suffer various trials, so that the genuineness of your faith, more precious than gold which though perishable is tested by fire, may redound to praise and glory and honor at the revelation of Jesus Christ (1 Pet 1:6-7).

The reasons for which we first embark on our journey of faith are often not the reasons that sustain us later in life. Many Christians, especially when they are younger, maintain their faith primarily because they were raised that way, because they haven't encountered reasons to consider alternatives, because they enjoy the social experience of their faith community, or for other reasons. There isn't anything intrinsically wrong with holding on to your faith for such reasons; in the absence of any serious trials or difficulties, it is easy for us to feel comfortable with the current state of our prayer life, our level of personal holiness and virtue, and the overall quality of our relationship with God. This comfort, however, can be dangerous because it can prevent us from having the sense of seriousness and urgency that we need in order to really grow in our faith. If God did not allow trials and suffering to enter our life, we would almost inevitably remain in this comfort zone, and never reach the greatness that He calls each of us to. Fortunately, while God loves us the way we are, He loves us too much to leave us that way, and so He does permit trials and suffering to enter our lives. When we begin to not only reluctantly accept these trials, but willingly enter into them and even in a sense choose them, we learn to align our will with the will of God, and become capable of enduring more and therefore loving more. In the process of achieving this endurance by perseverance, we begin to see our motivations transform. Until we reach the point when we truly love God above everything and everyone else, we will continue to need this process of purification. I personally experienced a profound insight into the need for this purification during the marathon, especially while running miles

22 through 25, which were by far the most difficult for me. The dead cliché "put one foot in front of the other" took on new life and for a time was almost my mantra.

Suffering + God = Hope

The triumph of the will over the senses, of the soul of the body, was so immediate and clear to me near the end of the race that it almost seemed as though I was outside of or over my body, commanding it the way a jockey commands a horse. At that point, my body and mind were both so exhausted that I had completely forgotten my original reasons for signing up for the marathon. I discovered that wanting a "personal challenge" or a "reason to get in better shape" offer no motivation or consolation whatsoever when you've been running for four hours. Had I not managed to replace these slogans with something far deeper and more enduring, then I would have found myself walking (or more realistically, limping) those last few miles. For me, the only thought which survived the hammer and anvil of the marathon was the conviction that the testing of my will in during the race was in some way connected to my spiritual commitment to God. Of course, not finishing the race would not have been be an actual spiritual failure or sin on my part. However, in my mind, I became convinced that by enduring the physical trial of the marathon I could prove to myself that, with God's help, I could endure great spiritual trials in the future as well. Therefore, when I did finally finish the race, I was infused with a heavy dose of hope in the future, and in my reflection was reminded of Saint Paul's words:

> [W]e rejoice in our hope of sharing the glory of God. More than that, we rejoice in our sufferings, knowing that suffering produces endurance, and endurance produces character, and character produces hope, and hope does not disappoint us, because God's love has been poured into our hearts through the Holy Spirit who has been given to us (Rom 5:2-5).

While every Christian obviously cannot complete a marathon for a variety of valid reasons, everyone can do something that seems far beyond their capacity, and that tests their will to the breaking point. I am convinced that this has tremendous spiritual benefit, and so I highly recommend that every Christian take on some challenge that achieves this purpose. You will become a more virtuous person and more aware of your dependence on God as a result. Thank you for reading, and may God bless you and inspire you to grow in every way possible! In the words of Pope Francis during his homily at the Mass in Washington, D.C., *"¡Siempre adelante!"* (Always forward!).

† Under the Mercy,

Chris Trummer

The Tongue is a Fire: The Importance of Striving for Purity of Speech

The Importance of Speech in Our Christian Faith

As Christians, speech and words are particularly meaningful to us for a variety of reasons. First of all (literally), we believe that God spoke all of Creation into being out of nothing: "For he spoke, and it came to be; he commanded, and it stood forth" (Psa 33:9). We believe that Jesus Christ is the Logos, that is, the Word of God: "In the beginning was the Word, and the Word was with God, and the Word was God" (Jn 1:1). We believe that Christ became incarnate at the moment when the Blessed Virgin Mary said, "Let it be done to me according to your word" (Lk 1:38). We believe that the Bible is the inspired Word of God. Due to the sacramental nature of the Catholic Faith, words are particularly meaningful to those of us who are Catholic Christians. Like other Christians, we believe that the words spoken at baptism are essential to the validity of the sacrament: "I baptize you in the name of the Father, and of the Son, and of the Holy Spirit." We believe that God works through human priests to forgive us of our sins in the Sacrament of Penance (Confession), using the words, "I absolve you of your sins in the name of the Father, and of the Son, and of the Holy Spirit." During the Mass, we believe that ordinary bread and wine are changed into the Body, Blood, Soul, and Divinity of Jesus Christ when the priest utters the words spoken by Christ at the Last Supper (Mt 26:26-28, Mk 14:22,24, Lk 22:19-20).

The Power of Speech

How great a forest is set ablaze by a small fire! (Js 3:5)

As human beings, we cannot speak things into existence out of nothing the way God can (which is probably a good thing). However, as creatures made in God's image and likeness, our speech does have creative power Like our actions, the words we speak are not only a reflection of our thoughts and inward disposition; they also have the power to change us, influence others, and praise and glorify God. Unfortunately, our speech doesn't always serve God, others, or ourselves in a positive way, but is at times destructive. Today, there is an epidemic of obscene language, profanity, gossip, hate speech, and abuse of the name of God. Sadly, these destructive acts of speech are often justified and even praised in the name of humor (one of our favorite idols). Personally, I used to be guilty of all these sins (especially profanity), and I still struggle with some of them on a regular basis. Having also noticed the prevalence of these problems among many other people as well, especially young people, I was moved to share my thoughts on this topic. Don't worry, I haven't forgot about Advent or Christmas—this topic has just been pressing my mind lately, and in fact, purifying our language is one way to make a beautiful gift of ourselves for Christ when He comes into our lives in a new way this Christmas.

> Who shall ascend the hill of the Lord?
> And who shall stand in his holy place?
> He who has clean hands and a pure heart,
> who does not lift up his soul to what is false,
> and does not swear deceitfully.
> He will receive blessing from the Lord,
> and vindication from the God of his salvation (Psa 24:3-5)

Don't Defile Yourself

> "What comes out of the mouth proceeds from the heart, and this defiles a man. For out of the heart come evil thoughts, murder, adultery, fornication, theft, false witness, slander" (Mt 15:18-19).

It is tempting to believe that the way we speak does not affect how we view other people or change our attitude towards life. However, nothing in our experience supports this notion. The reality is that our speech is closely connected to our beliefs, moods, and attitudes. This connection is reciprocal, because the person we are now is revealed in part by the way we speak, and the way we speak has a powerful effect on the person we become. It is easy enough to admit this in theory, but in practice it is much more difficult. How often do we say things in arguments, in moments of frustration or anger, or in jest that tear others down and defile us? How often do we justify vulgarity, perversion, gossip, and the verbal abuse of others for the sake of laughter? I frequently hear statements such as, "That's sooo bad! But it's really funny!" and "I'm going straight to hell for saying that!" (usually followed by more laughter, as if going to hell is a joking matter). Jesus Himself said that we will be judged on the content of our speech:

> I tell you, on the day of judgment men will render account for every careless word they utter; for by your words you will be justified, and by your words you will be condemned (Mt 12:36-37).

I don't know about you, but I find those words hard to read! Many people believe the modern lie that the morality of our actions, including our speech, is entirely dependent on the circumstances. This idea flows out of the pervasive moral relativism of our time, which Pope Emeritus Benedict XVI diagnosed as the most serious threat to our world. Regarding speech, this relativism is manifest in the belief that language itself is morally neutral, and that any idea we have that certain types of speech are morally wrong must be based entirely on whatever the prevailing social norms happen to be. I often hear people say things such as, "Don't say that around the kids!" This can be an expression of genuine concern, but it is often hypocrisy. If we don't expect or demand pure and respectful speech from adults, then why are we so worried that children might imitate them? After all, aren't our children supposed to be imitating us? The ideal we should strive for is that our speech is the same regardless of who might be within earshot.

The use of profanity amongst young people is little more than a rite of passage into adulthood. The majority of parents actually expect teenagers to start using profanity and impure language, and simply give up trying to prevent such speech once their children have reached the "appropriate" age (whatever that means). The idea that there is an appropriate age for profane or impure speech makes any attempt to condemn such speech on moral grounds unconvincing. For if an age-based standard is justified, then adults should be more accountable for their speech, not less, since they are more experienced and more aware of their influence on others. Instead of embracing the current eroded standard of speech, we should set a higher standard for ourselves and model this standard to others. As Saint Paul wrote, "Do not be conformed to this world but be transformed by the renewal of your mind, that you may prove what is the will of God, what is good and acceptable and perfect" (Rmn 12:2). I'm not simply suggesting that it would be nice if we could "clean things up a little" when it comes to our speech. Rather, I'm pointing out that purity of speech is a necessary virtue for Christians and a practical step to overcoming the negativity, perversity, and growing lack of respect for human dignity that plagues our culture and our world today.

Impart Grace to Others

> Let no evil talk come out of your mouths, but only such as is good for edifying, as fits the occasion, that it may impart grace to those who hear (Eph 4:29).

As people of faith, we cannot be content with baseness and impurity of speech simply because it prevails in the world around us. Instead, we should recognize that setting ourselves apart from the rest of the world, both in belief and in practice, is essential to bearing witness to the "Joy of the Gospel," as Pope Francis has invited each of us to do. One of the first things people notice when they meet you, after your appearance and body language, is your speech. If they don't hear you swearing, cutting down others, or using impure language, they will think to themselves, "There's something different about this person." This difference, this set-apart-ness (when you study philosophy, you quickly discover that "-ness" can be added to any word), is attractive to people and even contagious. It not only shows others that you take yourself seriously, but also that you recognize the great influence you have on others and care enough to speak in a manner that reflects this awareness. As Christians, we should always work to build others up by our words and actions. The more we allow profane, slanderous, and blasphemous language to become a regular part of our speech, the less effective we will be in this endeavor. If the words we use and the conversations we have contradict the values of our Christian faith, then we severely undermine our credibility as disciples of Jesus Christ. People can easily detect a lack of authenticity.

From the same mouth come blessing and cursing. My brethren, this ought not to be so. Does a spring pour forth from the same opening fresh water and brackish? . . . No more can salt water yield fresh (Js 3:10-12).

In All Things May God Be Glorified

Sadly, the name of God is constantly used in vain, in disrespect, and in outright blasphemy today. Worse yet, many of the people who frequently use God's name in vain also profess to be Christians. I've noticed that many Christians have a false understanding of what it means to use God's name "in vain." They often justify their misuse of God's name by saying, "Well, I didn't mean it," or "I was only joking." Such excuses are erroneous, because to do or say something "in vain" literally means "to no avail" or "without purpose." In other words, saying something in vain means that you didn't mean it. Any time you use God's name in a way that isn't deliberate, purposeful, or prayerful, you're using it in vain. The name of God should never be used as a means to the end of humor, and especially not in an expression of anger or frustration (e.g., saying "G.D."). Despite how common and seemingly harmless the expression "Oh my God" may be, this is also an abuse of God's name (outside of prayer, of course). I even hear many Christians using the name of Jesus, our Lord and Savior, in a flippant or outright disrespectful way. In his letter to the Philippians, Saint Paul writes, "at the name of Jesus every knee should bow, in heaven and on earth and under the earth" (Php 2:10). Following this declaration, the practice among Catholics of bowing one's head at the name of Jesus, especially during the Mass, used to be a common devotion. Many people still do this, and when I first learned about it (a couple of years ago), I found it beautiful and appropriate and so began doing it myself. This small devotion is a practical way to glorify God more in our speech, because it makes our use of His name more intentional and reverent. There is another simple and effective devotion that not only increases our respect for God in speech, but makes reparation for sins of blasphemy and profane language in the world: The Divine

Praises. A Jesuit priest originally composed the Divine Praises in the late 18th century. They are:

Blessed be God. Blessed be His Holy Name.
Blessed be Jesus Christ, true God and true Man.
Blessed be the Name of Jesus.
Blessed be His Most Sacred Heart.
Blessed be His Most Precious Blood.
Blessed be Jesus in the Most Holy Sacrament of the Altar.
Blessed be the Holy Spirit, the Paraclete.
Blessed be the great Mother of God, Mary most Holy.
Blessed be her Holy and Immaculate Conception.
Blessed be her Glorious Assumption.
Blessed be the name of Mary, Virgin and Mother.
Blessed be St. Joseph, her most chaste spouse.
Blessed be God in His Angels and in His Saints. Amen.

Think (and Speak!) About These Things

Our speech is NOT a morally neutral exercise of our tongue, but rather a reflection of who we are, an influence on who we become, a means of witnessing our faith to others, and above all, one of the primary ways in which we can glorify God as His beloved children. Recognizing this, we should strive and pray for purity in our speech and encourage this purity from everyone in our sphere of influence. Instead of allowing ourselves to be conformed to the childish, foolish, and impure ways of speaking that the world offers us as the "norm," we should take Jesus as our norm and allow His transforming grace into this most practical area of our lives. By doing this, we be more able to bear witness to our own dignity and the dignity of all people, impart grace to everyone we encounter, and glorify God in all that we do. Thank you for reading! God bless!

Finally, brethren, whatever is true, whatever is honorable, whatever is just, whatever is pure, whatever is lovely, whatever is gracious, if there is any excellence, if there is anything worthy of praise, think about these things (Php 4:8).

† Under the Mercy, Chris Trummer

160

Bearing the Full Weight of Reality: My Battle Through Alcohol to Freedom

I was 16 years old and a sophomore in high school when I got drunk for the first time. You might think that vomiting repeatedly, blacking out, and spending the next day nursing a hangover (without even knowing what a hangover was) would have been enough to deter me from binge drinking again. Unfortunately, it wasn't. Instead, that night started me down a dark road of pain, confusion, and sin, which severely hindered and delayed my ability to develop into a complete person capable of authentic and loving relationships. I traveled down that road for about 6 years, and it wasn't until June of last year that I finally allowed God to deliver me out of my slavery to alcohol and into the freedom of sobriety. My intention in telling the story of my liberation and in reflecting on the dangers of alcohol is not to demonize alcohol, nor to condemn anyone who chooses to partake of it. Rather, I simply want to share with others the story of how God has worked a miracle in my life by doing for me what I never could have done for myself. It is gratitude and sincere concern that compel me, not guilt or a desire to judge others. That being said, if you or anyone you know struggles with alcohol or other substance abuse, please be open to what God may be asking you to do. He desires only your ultimate good, happiness, and freedom.

False Power and Freedom

For many people, alcohol is treated more as a tool than a beverage. Specifically, it is used as a catalyst in social situations to produce an environment with less tension, awkwardness, and inhibitions. This is why alcohol is affectionately referred to by some as "liquid courage". Because alcohol is a depressant, it is indeed very effective at creating a relaxed and care-free atmosphere, one that is more conducive to fun, pleasure, and ease of interaction between people, especially strangers. This feature of alcohol makes it particularly attractive to young people, who are burdened with the two-fold task of understanding their own identity and learning how to successfully relate to others. I was personally enthralled when I discovered the "super powers" alcohol seemed to grant me. Being an introverted and overly self-conscious guy, I found the opportunity to transform into a confident, charismatic, and spontaneous person at will to be both exhilarating and addicting.

Within a couple of months of my first taste of this new found glory, I was hooked. From that point on, my primary social concern was obtaining alcohol and consuming it with my friends. At first, we encountered the problem of having no place to drink, since none of our parents were okay with the idea of teenage boys binge drinking (oppressive, I know). Our solution to this problem was to exercise our other newly acquired freedom: driving. Apparently, the statistics we were told in driver's education class and stories from motivational speakers about how they had barely survived drunk driving accidents had not been enough to convince our teenage minds that we were anything less than invincible. We would drink and drive around on back country roads with a 30 pack of beer in the trunk and our music blaring, stopping frequently to retrieve more cans and to "water" the ditch alongside the road. Eventually though, we were able to upgrade to drinking at an older friend's college apartment or at the house of a friend whose parents were away. I would let nothing stand in the way of me having a good time with my friends. I would lie to my parents about where I was and who I was with; I would steal bottles of liquor from stores; my friends and I went so far as to sneak cases of beer into the movie theater. Alcohol had to be part of the equation whenever possible, and we found social events without it to be painfully boring. Ironically, it was really ourselves that we were bored with.

So what exactly was it about this shallow, unhealthy, and reckless lifestyle that attracted me and the majority of my high school classmates to it? What did we at least perceive to be good and worthwhile in drinking alcohol, especially in light of the potential legal consequences and obvious risks involved? Certainly the carefree and light-hearted atmosphere that intoxication produces attracted us, as I mentioned before. However, my ongoing reflection on this puzzling question has led me to suspect that the appeal of alcohol stems from much deeper issues in human beings. Most of these issues are distortions of perfectly legitimate and even noble desires that we all share, such as our desire for intimacy with others, both the intimacy of friendship and romantic intimacy. Other issues arise in

162

response to struggles such as existential frustration and anxiety about our lives and identity.

Hacking Intimacy

All human beings desire intimacy. This desire, as with any other natural desire, is expressed in a variety of ways, depending on the person and the relationship or situation. There is the obvious yet profound example of intimacy between a man and a woman in love. But other examples of intimacy abound; there is intimacy between parents and their children, between close friends, between counselors and their patients, between spiritual directors and their directees, and even between teachers and their students. All of these can be healthy expressions of human intimacy. As Christians, we believe that our need and desire for intimacy comes from our being created *imago Dei* (in the image of God), Who is a Trinity of persons sharing perfect intimacy through an eternal exchange of love. As human beings, however, our finite and fallen nature creates obstacles to intimacy, such as pride, lust, and envy. That is why when Adam and Eve first sinned, their intimate relationship with God was broken and they hid from God, which prompted God to ask, "Where are you?" (Gen 3:9). God was not asking for Adam's physical whereabouts (He already knew that); God was asking Adam where he was in relation to Himself. When we encounter obstacles to intimacy in our own lives, we are forced to either work to overcome them and experience the intimacy we need and desire, or else give up on this enterprise and resign ourselves to a lonely existence devoid of interpersonal depth.

However, there is a third option, and that is to try to "hack" intimacy by bypassing the obstacles to it. This is the method that so often enlists the help of alcohol. When we choose to become intoxicated with others as a means of achieving intimacy with them, several things inevitably happen as a result. First, alcohol does not only thin your blood, it also thins your personality. Alcohol is not a selective depressant; it depresses (and as a result, suppresses) everything about your personality that makes you unique. This includes negative features, such as awkwardness, uptightness, anxiety, fear, hesitation, and excessive self-consciousness. It also suppresses positive features, such as prudence, self-control, vigilance, emotional depth, clarity of thought, and self-awareness. By diluting these features, alcohol mitigates the characteristics of human beings that can often make interaction, conversation, and relationships intimidating and challenging. The downside of this is that it also ensures that your interactions, conversations, and relationships will be shallower. By minimizing the uniqueness and individuality of each human person, alcohol often prevents us from presenting our true selves *to* the other, and from learning to see and appreciate what is intrinsically lovable *in* the other. In a sense, it eliminates some of the messiness involved when different personalities come together in favor of a kind of "lowest common denominator", in which each person's "edges" are rounded off. It levels the playing field by bringing everyone down to a mediocre level.

When people become incapable of relating to others and enjoying their company, unless alcohol is part of the equation, what does that reveal about them? Implicitly, the person who has reached this point is saying by their actions, "If people knew me, the *real* me, they would either not understand me, not accept me, or not really love me. Therefore, I need to subdue my real self in order to become acceptable to others." An inability or unwillingness to relate to others without alcohol may also reveal that the person does not see others, in their deepest selves, as worth getting to actually know. If experiencing the full reality of a person inspires our interest, appreciation, and love, then alcohol cannot enhance this experience. In fact, it can only diminish it, because it conceals the fullness of human personality. When alcohol is introduced into human interactions and relationships, it produces a false sense of intimacy and mutual understanding. This is why "drinking buddies" are rarely close friends who really know each other in an authentic way. It is also why some one seeking to use another person for selfish pleasure, as in the case of a "one-night stand", is far more likely to buy that person a drink than to enter into a personal and meaningful conversation. That action effectively says, "I'm not interested in *you*. I'm interested in getting *you* out of the way so that I can have access to *your body*." This is the basic mentality underlying the hook-up culture today, and frankly, it is pathetic. Animals are supposed to "hook up"; men and women are supposed to love each other.

Diversion

> "The only thing that consoles us for our miseries is diversion. And yet it is the greatest of our miseries. For it is that above all which prevents us thinking about ourselves and leads us imperceptibly to destruction." — Blaise Pascal, *Pensées*

Alcohol can also contribute to the epidemic of diversion that plagues our world today. When I speak of diversion, I'm referring to the tendency of people to occupy themselves with endless stimuli, entertainment, and distractions in an effort, conscious or unconscious, to avoid facing questions of ultimate meaning and responsibility. In hindsight, I realize that this sort of diversion was an essential feature of my problem with alcohol. When fundamental questions about the meaning of my life arose, especially the question of whether or not there even was a meaning, I was too afraid to grapple with them, and so I simply tried to ignore them. Of course, one cannot avoid facing reality forever. Therefore, since I couldn't resolve my own uncertainties, nor could I ignore them indefinitely, I chose to disengage from reality in various ways—music, movies, video games, and alcohol being among my most trusted methods. I was like a child who, upon realizing he is no good at a game, simply refuses to play it. I thought that I was no good at life—with growing up, making friends, and handling social situations—and so I refused to participate. How sadly ironic it is when people refer to their constant need to escape reality as "living life to the full," when more often than not, such people are living a life of mediocrity and dissatisfaction. How reassuring then is Christ's response to this delusion: "I came that they may have life, and have it abundantly" (Jn 10:10).

Freely Chosen Slavery

A final negative consequence of alcohol abuse is its effects on the will, both immediate and long term. The immediate effect of alcohol on the will is well known and obvious. Alcohol directly impairs the human faculty of free will, which is a gift from God that separates us from animals, allowing us to make moral judgments, and making it possible for us to love. That is why choosing to become intoxicated or otherwise impairing your free will is a serious sin. Drunkenness makes us highly susceptible to other sins, distorts our identity as creatures made in the image and likeness of God, and destroys our freedom as His children. Unfortunately, many people enjoy drinking for the very reason that it weakens their will. This is usually done in an effort to absolve themselves of their moral responsibility. However, the excuse, "I was drunk" is invalid if you deliberately got drunk in order to overcome the resistance of your conscience. In Catholic moral theology, full consent of the will is required for an action to be mortally (i.e., seriously) sinful. However, while a person may not have full consent of the will while intoxicated, their freely made decision to surrender their freedom is itself a serious sin. That is why Saint Paul wrote that drunkards will not inherit the kingdom of God (1 Cor 6:10). Sometimes we minimize passages such as this to justify our behavior, but you couldn't ask for a more straightforward teaching.

The long-term effect of alcohol on the human will is a direct consequence of the immediate or short-term effect. This is the weakening of the will against temptation and sin. Over time, the repeated decision to forfeit one's free will begins to numb the conscience. The more often you choose to temporarily dispense with morality for the sake of pleasure, the more morality itself will begin to seem dispensable. If you decide to make exceptions to your moral duties and obligations—say, on Friday and Saturday nights for example—then you will soon find yourself treating morality as relative or merely provisional. You will start seeing morality as elective, something that is chosen, instead of something objective and foundational to reality. This is a deadly trap, one that our current pope, following the teaching of his last two predecessors, has warned against with profound seriousness. To avoid this trap of moral laxity and indifference, let's heed the advice of our first pope, Saint Peter, who wrote: "Be sober, be watchful. Your adversary the devil prowls around like a roaring lion, seeking some one to devour" (1 Pet 5:8).

Placing EVERYTHING Under the Mercy

By the time I entered seminary nearly three years ago now, I believed my alcohol consumption to be totally under control, and my problems with it to be a thing of the past. At the beginning of summer last year, I discovered that I was presumptuous and mistaken. During my first couple of weeks living at a parish rectory, I found myself somewhat depressed and avoiding most social situations, opting instead to spend my nights reading or watching movies and drinking alcohol by myself at the rectory. To my surprise, I found myself incapable of stopping at just one or two drinks, and I drank far too much on multiple occasions, even after telling myself I would dial back the amount I drank. I was greatly disappointed in myself, but wasn't fully aware of the gravity of my situation until I received what I am convinced was a powerful grace from God, which gave me insight into my weakness and my desperate need for Him in this matter. I was in adoration before the Blessed Sacrament, and was praying as sincerely as I've ever prayed. I asked God to show me what I needed to do to be free from what had by that time clearly become a serious problem. Suddenly, I had a moment of *extreme* clarity, during which I saw myself as having only two options: 1) to live the rest of my life struggling with alcohol and trying, unsuccessfully, to negotiate and compromise with this destructive force in my life, or 2) to abandon alcohol completely. God was not offering me a third way. Until that moment, I had been clinging to alcohol as a vestige of my former self, something other than God that I could occasionally return to as a momentary escape and take refuge in if I felt the need. However, I finally realized that in trying to escape my problems using alcohol, I had really been avoiding God and His invitation to trust Him with everything, even this thing, this shameful and embarrassing part of my life. After hovering between the two choices for a moment in hesitation, I finally surrendered myself, and in doing so received a peace that I had never known, a "peace which passes all understanding" (Php 4:7).

In that moment, I became perfectly content to finally let go of my past life, to "put off the old nature with its practices" and "put on the new nature" (Col 3:9-10). Since that day, June 7th, 2015, I have by the grace of God remained completely sober. What's most astonishing to me is that I have never even experienced a serious temptation to drink again, despite my past attempts to temporarily quit drinking being short-lived and full of strong temptations. I now live with a new and profound sense of freedom, knowing that I don't have to constantly worry about alcohol and the damage it could have inflicted, not only on myself, but also on all the people around me, including those whom I will (God willing) serve someday in the future as a priest. Instead of trying to manipulate or dilute my personality in order to meet what I perceive to be the expectations of others, I am now content to let God form me into the man He created me to be, which far exceeds anything I could ever imagine or aspire to on my own. I am committed to placing myself, my *whole* self, under the mercy of God, because therein lies my only hope.

Choose Freedom, Choose God

Let us all choose the freedom that belongs to us as children of God, and in doing so, embrace the full weight of reality that He wants us to experience, as a means of growing closer to others, and above all, closer to Himself. What this choice of freedom entails will be different for each person. I am certainly *not* suggesting that everyone needs to avoid alcohol altogether simply because I discovered this to be necessary for me. However, I *am* suggesting that all of us be honest enough with ourselves and with God to identify whatever obstacles stand in the way of our freedom. If one of those obstacles is alcohol or another drug, then of course, we need to take courage and bring that before the Lord, preferably beginning with the Sacrament of Reconciliation. God wants all of us to experience true intimacy with others, and ultimately, with Himself. Why should we delay the pursuit of this any longer?

> . . . you know what hour it is, how it is full time now for you to wake from sleep. For salvation is nearer to us now than when we first believed; the night is far gone, the day is at hand. Let us then cast off the works of darkness and put on the armor of light; let us conduct ourselves becomingly as in the day, not in reveling and drunkenness, not in debauchery and licentiousness, not in quarreling and jealousy. But put on the Lord Jesus Christ, and make no provision for the flesh, to gratify its desires (Rom 13:11-14).

Thank you for reading this rather long post! May God bless you and guide you into a greater freedom, and as a result, into a deeper intimacy with others and Himself.

168

† Under the Mercy,

Chris Trummer

Encountering God's Existence: The Uncaused Cause

Anyone who has spent time around young children is aware of their tendency to ask the question, "Why?" Often times, this tendency can shift from comical to slightly irritating, especially when every answer you provide is immediately followed by yet another, "But why?" This curiosity, while it may seem silly at times to us older humans, is actually an innocent and productive example of the human desire to know. As soon as we become aware of cause and effect relationships, we develop a strong desire to know the cause behind every given effect. Unlike other animals, we do not simply react to our environment, but seek to understand it. We are not content with knowing *that* something happens in nature, we want to know *why* it happens. This desire to know the causes of things is the basis for all scientific and philosophical inquiry, and in fact, all rational inquiry. Moreover, the predictive ability of scientific theories, which is a key element in assessing their validity, takes for granted that an effect proper to a cause will happen necessarily. As human beings, our desire to know things on a deeper, metaphysical level (e.g., the causes behind events) is what separates us from other, non-rational, animals. Consider that when an animal has all of its biological needs met, it almost invariably goes into an inactive state or sleeps. By contrast, when a human being has all of its biological needs met, it begins to ask questions, questions whose answers do not pertain to any strictly biological need, such as: Why am I here? Where did I come from? Where am I going? What is the purpose of my life? What is the purpose of life altogether? And, the most sublime question of all: *Why is there something rather than nothing?*

I Demand an Explanation!

Whether in the simple events of our daily lives or in the most complex experiments in the laboratory, our experience of the natural world tells us that reality is completely intelligible, that is, that every coherent question about reality has an answer. Stated more simply, for every effect, there is a cause. Given adequate observation, we see (and indeed, even predict) that every observable phenomenon has a sufficient explanation for its occurrence. Reality is not absurd. Even when the cause of something is extremely difficult to assess, we never give up and assume that the event in question is simply a brute fact of nature that we must accept, something that "just happens". No, even if conclude that we may never know how or why a particular event occurs, we consign this to our human or technological limitations, because we know that there *must* be a cause, an explanation. This demand that every event have a sufficient explanation, that every effect have a cause, is an unavoidable fact of rational thought. In philosophy, it is known as the *principle of sufficient reason.* Rather than simply guiding our search for answers to our practical and scientific questions, we can quite easily apply this principle to questions of metaphysics (i.e., the study of fundamental reality beyond mere matter). "Does God exist?" is one such question, and it is to this that we now turn.

Looks Like Someone Should Have Bought a Kindle...

The following is a simple thought experiment about the nature of cause and effect relationships. Suppose that you want to check out a book from your local library. Excited, you go there to do so, but you soon learn from the librarian that they don't have the book in stock, and will have to borrow it from another library through an inter-library loan. "Okay," you say to the librarian, "so I assume the book will be here in a few days then?" "Actually no," he responds, "because the library we're ordering the book from has to order it from another library first." Slightly disappointed, you ask, "Oh, so it will be more like a week or so before it arrives?" Checking the computer again with a confused glance, he apologizes, "I'm sorry but no, the book won't be here in a week either because apparently that second library has to first order it from *another* library." At this point, you're starting to get annoyed and to doubt that you will ever see the book that you're anxious to read. Then the librarian tells you something very strange, in fact, it's so strange that it makes no sense to you at all and you assume that he must be playing a prank on you. He says, "I'm so sorry, but it turns out that the number of libraries that need to first borrow the book before lending it to us is actually *infinite.*" If we excuse for now the impossibility of a literally infinite number of libraries existing on the planet for the sake of our thought experiment, what can we still say about the possibility of you ever receiving your (apparently extremely rare) book? It's not a trick question. The answer is: zero, zilch, none.

Job Opening: Cause of All Reality

This might seem intuitively obvious, but let's examine this answer a little closer. Why would you never receive the book? The answer is, because an infinite number of libraries that all need to borrow a book before being able to lend can never provide the book. So, what do books and libraries have to do with God's existence? Well, in our scenario above, what would be required in order for you to check out the book? Of course, there would have to be a library that actually *has* the book in stock, one that doesn't have to borrow the book from another library. No matter how many libraries you add to the scenario, if they *all* have to borrow the book before lending it, then the book will never reach you. Now, switch gears and imagine that "existence" is the book in the scenario. What do we know about you? You exist (you have the book). Did you always exist? No, you were born *x* number of years ago. Why do you exist then? Because your parents conceived you, gave birth to you, and cared for you. But why do they exist? Because their parents did the same for them. But why do *their* parents exist? Because their parents . . . You can probably guess where this is going. If we could keep going back far enough with our questions and answers, we would eventually reach the first human beings as the explanation for why you exist, and beyond them, whatever creatures might have preceded them, and beyond those creatures, whatever environmental causes were needed to bring about their existence, and beyond those causes, whatever causes were needed to bring the Earth into existence, and so on and so on, all the way back to the Big Bang (assuming for now that the Big Bang marks the beginning of the universe as most physicists and cosmologists believe). Well then, where does God fit into this (condensed) narrative of the history of physical reality? Remember what we said about the libraries—there must exist a library that actually *has* the book in order for you to receive it. But you *do* have the book, you exist right now. That means that something must exist in reality that caused you to exist (through an extremely long and complicated series of other causes), *without needing to be caused itself.* This means that there must exist an "uncaused cause" in reality.

Wait, This Sounds Familiar...

Okay, what's the big deal? So there has to be an uncaused cause, but that could be anything, right? It doesn't have to be something like God, does it? Actually, when we think about what it means for something to be "uncaused", some interesting implications quickly surface. For one thing, in order for something to be uncaused, it would have to be eternal, that is, outside of time. This is because something that is uncaused could not have begun to exist at some past point in time, since the beginning of its existence (i.e., its creation) would require a cause. Also, as the only uncaused cause, it would have to be the cause, explanation, or creator of everything else that exists (i.e., all the "caused causes). Finally, an uncaused cause would have to be immaterial (i.e., not made of matter), because things that are made of matter are composed in a certain form, which requires a cause, and subject to change (which is a measured by time). So, in order for you and your iPhone and your dog and the Statue of Liberty and penguins and black holes and everything and everyone else to exist, there must be an immaterial (a.k.a. spiritual), eternal, and uncaused cause. What (or Who) does that sound like? In the words of Saint Thomas Aquinas, "And this everyone calls God."

† Under the Mercy,

Chris Trummer

The Faith That is Sacramental

One of the most significant theological differences between the Catholic Faith and most Protestant traditions lies in the amount of emphasis given to sacraments. In the Catholic Church we recognize seven sacraments, whereas most Protestant traditions today recognize only two. The two that are common to Catholics and Protestants alike are Baptism and the Eucharist or "communion." The seven sacraments that the Catholic Church acknowledges and celebrates are: Baptism, Confirmation, Eucharist, Penance (or Reconciliation), the Anointing of the Sick, Holy Orders, and Matrimony. In the Catholic Church, reception of the sacraments is central to living the fulness of the Christian faith. Considering how essential the role of the sacraments is, it is important for us to understand what a sacrament is, why the Christian faith is sacramental, and why the Catholic Church teaches the necessity of the sacraments for salvation and sanctification.

What is a Sacrament?

What is a sacrament? First of all the Catholic Church considers herself to be *the* sacrament of salvation: "The Church in this world is the sacrament of salvation, the sign and the instrument of the communion of God and men" (CCC 780). It is from this understanding of the Church as sacrament that the particular sacraments within the Church derive their meaning. There is no clearer definition of the sacraments than that found in the *Catechism of the Catholic Church:*

> The sacraments are efficacious signs of grace, instituted by Christ and entrusted to the Church, by which divine life is dispensed to us. The visible rites by which the sacraments are celebrated signify and make present the graces proper to each sacrament. They bear fruit in those who receive them with the required dispositions" (*CCC* 1131).

This definition contains a lot of important information, so let's unpack it a little. First, the sacraments are *signs*, which means that they represent and point to a reality beyond themselves. However, the sacraments are not merely signs because they are *efficacious,* meaning they actually bring about a real change in the person who receives them. This one word, *efficacious,* has immense theological implications, because the failure to acknowledge the efficacious nature of the sacraments produces radically different (and incorrect) understandings of them. A paradigm example of this is the sacrament of Baptism. In the Catholic Church, we believe in "baptismal regeneration," which means that Baptism is necessary for salvation because it actually cleanses our souls of Original Sin and dispenses sanctifying grace into our souls. This is not simply a symbolic or semantic way of describing an interior process of conversion, because it marks an objective change in reality independent of our mind or conviction. In the words of Saint Peter, "Baptism...now saves you...as an appeal to God for a clear conscience, through the resurrection of Jesus Christ" (1 Pet 3:21).

Born Again—the Bible Way

Many Christians will speak of the need for every person to be "born again," something that Catholics also believe. However, when we speak of being "born again," we're referring primarily to Baptism, as Christ himself did. When Nicodemus spoke to Jesus, marveling at the signs he was performing, Jesus said to him: "Truly, truly, I say to you, unless one is born anew, he cannot see the kingdom of God" (Jn 3:3). Hence the necessity of being born again. However, Jesus did not stop at these words. Nicodemus, perplexed at the idea of being "born again," proceeded to ask Jesus, "How can a man be born when he is old? Can he enter a second time into his mother's womb and be born?" (v. 4) Apart from the rather comical idea of taking this question literally lies the essential question: "How?" Nicodemus was surely thinking, "If this wise man from God tells me I must be born again, then knowing what I must do to achieve this rebirth is of utmost importance." Curiously, many Protestants, if asked what it means to be born again, will respond with something along the lines of, "You have to ask Jesus to come into your heart and accept him as your personal Lord and Savior" (this process is sometimes referred to as praying the "Sinner's Prayer"). I say this is curious not only because Protestants tend to be well versed in Sacred Scripture, but primarily because Jesus himself told us exactly how to be born again, and he didn't mention praying any such prayer. Instead, he said to Nicodemus, "Truly, truly, I say to you, unless one is born of *water and the Spirit*, he cannot enter the kingdom of God" (v. 5, emphasis added). What did Jesus mean by "water and the Spirit"? Well, what did he just get done doing prior to this encounter? The synoptic gospels record it: "...when Jesus was baptized, he went up immediately from the water, and behold, the heavens were opened and he saw the Spirit of God descending like a dove, and alighting on him" (Mt 3:16). Here we see that water and the Spirit are joined together in the action of baptism.

There is nothing wrong *whatsoever* with asking Jesus to come into your heart and accepting him as your personal Lord and Savior; these are good and holy things that *all* Christians should do. However, when it comes to the question of being "born again," the sacrament of Baptism is the Biblical and historical way of doing that. This understanding of Baptism (and all the sacraments) as an action of God that brings about an objective change in the person who receives it is the basis for Catholics, along with several mainline Protestant denomination, practicing infant Baptism. The objection that one must be old enough to freely choose Baptism for oneself is rendered erroneous by the counterexample of offering Baptism to mentally handicapped persons who often lack the cognitive capacity to have any explicit understanding of the Gospel and to make such a decision for themselves. Consider also the many cases in which Jesus healed sick or possessed people at the request of others, such as the servant of the centurion (Mt 8:5-13). God may not impart grace to those who explicitly reject his will, but he certainly can and does to those who are at least open to him, with or without their explicit knowledge.

Matter Matters

"Shower, O heavens, from above,
and let the skies rain down righteousness;
let the earth open, that salvation may sprout forth,
and let it cause righteousness to spring up also;
I the LORD have created it" (Isa 45:8).

We have seen that the sacraments actually *do* something, and that they are not merely flashy outward signs or man-made formalities used to represent an interior conversion that has already taken place apart from the sacraments. Another important element of the sacraments is that most of them involve the use of material things: water in Baptism, and various oils in the other sacraments, for example. As in the sacrament of Baptism, the other sacraments use material following the example and command of Christ, who frequently used the physical things of the world when performing miracles and healing. For example, he used water to create wine at the wedding feast in Cana (Jn 2:1-11). Obviously, Jesus could have instead simply filled the jars with wine created out of nothing, but instead, he preferred to use already existing water. Likewise, in the case of the "man born blind" (Jn 9), Jesus could have simply said to the man, "See!" and he would have instantly been cured. Instead, Jesus mixed dirt with his spit and anointed the man with it, and then told him to wash in a pool of water (Jn 9:6-7). Why the use of dirt and water to accomplish this healing work? The reason is twofold. First, God created everything that exists and is glorified by his creation. In Genesis, we read that God "God saw everything that he had made, and behold, it was very good" (Gen 1:31). Since all matter is created good, God wills to make use of it, not only for accomplishing pragmatic purposes (like feeding us!), but even in his plan of salvation (the Cross began as an ordinary tree and became an instrument of salvation). He could have created us as purely spiritual beings without bodies (like the angels), but he didn't; he gave us physical bodies and a material world to inhabit. God is not a gnostic.

Divine Infiltration

The sacramental nature of the Catholic-Christian faith does not make sense apart from the Incarnation of God in the person of Jesus Christ. While God created the material universe as "good" and ordered it to serve the needs of human beings, matter itself has no inherent power to sanctify or communicate grace. (Otherwise, we would be seeing "spit and dirt therapy" advertisements instead of Lasik.) The natural world, being inseparably tied to the destiny of human beings as the apex of God's Creation, must likewise be "redeemed" in a sense before it can serve so noble a cause as the sanctification of the creatures created *imago Dei* (in the image of God). Saint Paul observed this:

> ...creation waits with eager longing for the revealing of the sons of God; for the creation was subjected to futility, not of its own will but by the will of him who subjected it in hope; because the creation itself will be set free from its bondage to decay and obtain the glorious liberty of the children of God. We know that the whole creation has been groaning in travail together until now (Rom 8:19-22).

Jesus Christ sanctified the natural world when he became a human being. The Incarnation pays a sort of "divine compliment" to Creation. Think again of Jesus' baptism in the Jordan River. As John the Baptist rightly objected, Jesus did not need to be baptized: "I need to be baptized by you, and do you come to me?" (Mt 3:14). Jesus' response tells us why he still willed to be baptized: "Let it be so now; for thus it is fitting for us to fulfill all righteousness" (v. 15). Notice that he says "to fulfill *all* righteousness." This point is crucial. We know that the whole purpose in Jesus' life, death, and resurrection is to redeem all of us (Jn 3:16-17). We also know that Jesus himself was without sin and thus had no need of redemption (Heb 4:15). Therefore, his desire to be baptized in order to "fulfill all righteousness" *must* be for our sake, for our redemption. Jesus was not baptized to be sanctified by the waters of Baptism, but so that the waters of Baptism would be sanctified by him. He did not negate John's baptism or render it obsolete, but *elevated* it to the status of a sacrament. In fact, it could be said that everything Jesus did on earth was an elevation or sanctification of what came before. His last words in scripture testify to this: "Behold, I make all things new" (Rev 21:5). Death itself was not immune to Christ's transformative power, since he changed it from a bitter finality of defeat and extinction of meaning into the very doorway by which we enter into eternal joy and fulfillment. As the words of an old oratorio (hymn) proclaim: "Thou hast made death glorious and triumphant, for through its portals we enter into the presence of the living God."

Seeing Sacramentally

The Catholic Church's focus on the sacramental nature of Christianity is justified not only by the goodness of the material world as created by God, but by her Savior's entrance into it, by which it has been sanctified and subordinated to God's plan of salvation. As Christians, we know that the Incarnation was not merely a past reality that a few thousand people were lucky enough to enjoy this side of heaven. Instead, it was the beginning of the kingdom of God, the kingdom that starts *here and now:* "Behold, the kingdom of God is in the midst of you" (Lk 17:21). When Jesus said, "I am with you always, to the close of the age," (Mt 28:20) he surely didn't mean that in a merely sentimental or analogical sense—He is *with* us always, in all his incarnate and tangible glory. The way in which he is most concretely present to us is in the sacraments of his Church, his Bride. Jesus established the New Covenant in his Body and Blood, which he offered on the cross and commanded his apostles to make present again in the Eucharist: "Do this in remembrance of me" (Lk 22:19, 1 Co 11:24). Christian faith always calls us to see things differently, to see everything in the light of God and his love for us. In Christ we see God differently, we see each other differently, we see ourselves differently; we even see Creation differently. As C.S. Lewis wrote: "I believe in Christianity as I believe that the sun has risen: not only because I see it, but because by it I see everything else." As Christians we also recognize that Creation is not some spiritually neutral medium of exchange in which we are "stuck" for now, awaiting a later time when we can escape from it. Rather, it is the product of God's love for us and an important means by which God wills to communicate his grace to us. Are the sacraments really necessary, considering they are temporal realities that take place in the finite material world? In the absolute sense, no. God can accomplish his plan of salvation by whatever means he chooses. Are they necessary for us? As necessary as the physical blood and water which gushed forth from the heart of Christ on Calvary two thousand years ago.

> *There flowed from his side water and blood.* Beloved, do not pass over this mystery without thought; it has yet another hidden meaning, which I will explain to you. I said that water and blood symbolized baptism and

the holy eucharist. From these two sacraments the Church is born: from baptism, *the cleansing water that gives rebirth and renewal through the Holy Spirit*, and from the holy eucharist. Since the symbols of baptism and the Eucharist flowed from his side, it was from his side that Christ fashioned the Church, as he had fashioned Eve from the side of Adam Moses gives a hint of this when he tells the story of the first man and makes him exclaim: *Bone from my bones and flesh from my flesh!* As God then took a rib from Adam's side to fashion a woman, so Christ has given us blood and water from his side to fashion the Church. God took the rib when Adam was in a deep sleep, and in the same way Christ gave us the blood and the water after his own death. Do you understand, then, how Christ has united his bride to himself and what food he gives us all to eat? By one and the same food we are both brought into being and nourished. As a woman nourishes her child with her own blood and milk, so does Christ unceasingly nourish with his own blood those to whom he himself has given life (From the *Catecheses* by Saint John Chrysostom, Office of Readings for Good Friday).

Signs of the Holy

The Catholic Church is often criticized as being excessively elaborate and showy in her liturgical celebrations. However, everything that goes into the Mass and other liturgies has a specific purpose, namely, to draw our minds deeper into the mysteries in which we are participating. We are each a unity of body and soul. Therefore, just as we do not experience and engage the world with our minds alone, but also with our bodies and all our sensory faculties, so too our worship of God is enriched when we incorporate more than just our minds. This is why the Catholic liturgy includes elements such as: music, vestments, candles, incense, bells, and changes in posture. It is not empty show—it is all carefully thought out to elevate our experience and foster our active participation. We are not passive observers who attend Church only in order to be entertained or moved, to "watch" what is happening there. No. We are *active* participants who are called to worship God together in the way that he has called us to worship him. The sacraments of the Church impart God's grace to us, so that we can be initiated, healed, strengthened, and conformed to the will of God in our lives. If we want to become the people God calls us to be, then we ought to gratefully take advantage of the tools he has given us to accomplish that task. The sacraments are those tools: time-tested and saint-approved.

† Under the Mercy,

Chris Trummer

Sources:

Catholic Biblical Association (Great Britain). *The Holy Bible: Revised Standard Version, Catholic Edition.* New York: National Council of Churches of Christ in the USA, 1994.

Catholic Church. *Catechism of the Catholic Church.* 2nd Ed. Washington, DC: United States Catholic Conference, 2000.

Catholic Church. *The Liturgy of the Hours According to the Roman Rite.* Volume II, Lenten and Easter Season. New York: Catholic Book Publishing Corp., 1976.

Admiratio et Humilitas: What the Seat of Wisdom Can Teach Lovers of Wisdom

Though she is but one, she can do all things, and while remaining in herself, she renews all things; in every generation she passes into holy souls and makes them friends of God, and prophets; for God loves nothing so much as the man who lives with wisdom (Wis 7:27-28).

Where is the Love?

The understanding of philosophy as the "love of wisdom" is greatly lost on the modern world. The existence of a separate philosophy "department" in most colleges and universities today is evidence of this, because one would think that the reason for studying any subject is to become wise in it. To understand philosophy as a distinct and specialized discipline, one limited to its own 'set' or 'type' of questions, is both a great error and a tragedy. The outspoken atheist, Richard Dawkins, exemplified this understanding of philosophy when, during a discussion, he was asked a question about the meaning of life and responded, "It's not a question that deserves an answer. The correct answer is: don't ask such a silly question." It is this narrow definition of philosophy which has fueled the separation between it and the natural sciences, and which leads to intellectual pitfalls such as positivism, pragmatism, and scientism, as Pope Saint John Paul II outlined so clearly in his Encyclical Letter, *Fides et Ratio*.

Whereas it once enjoyed status as the foundation of all other areas of human learning and knowledge, today philosophy has been reduced and caricatured to such an extent that many people (if not the majority) see it as abstract and lofty at best, and irrelevant or useless at worst. Why is this? What explains the widespread abuse of, and in some cases, complete disregard for, the "love of wisdom," philosophy? In other words, where is the love? There are undoubtedly numerous historical, social, intellectual, and even spiritual causes that could be cited as contributing factors to this phenomenon. However, I believe the two most significant factors are 1) a lack of wonder or awe, and 2) a lack of humility. This is where the Blessed Virgin Mary can serve as both our model and guide. Let us now consider how φιλοσοφία, "the love of wisdom," can learn from *Sedes Sapientiæ,* "the Seat of Wisdom."

Wonder: The Origin of All Philosophy

True wonder is innocent and genuine, like the curiosity of a child. It in fact begins in childhood, as anyone who has spent time around children knows from the number of times she or he has heard the question, "Why?" The questioning wonder of a child should be treasured and aspired to, because it is pure—free of any agenda or selfish motives—and because it is productive. It is also completely different from skepticism, which is usually motivated by pride or despair, instead of the humility and hope that accompany the inquiry founded on a basic trust in reality. It is this sense of trust, wonder, and openness that Jesus must of had in mind when he said, "Truly, I say to you, unless you turn and become like children, you will never enter the kingdom of heaven" (Mt 18:3). Not "like children" in terms of our reasoning, as Saint Paul explicitly exhorted the Corinthians to avoid: "Brethren, do not be children in your thinking; be babes in evil, but in thinking be mature" (1 Cor 14:20).

The Blessed Virgin Mary perfectly captures the combination of childlike wonder and mature thinking. After hearing about God's plan for her to conceive and bear a son, Mary sought to understand the will of God with greater clarity, and asked, "How shall this be, since I have no husband?" (Lk 1:34). Ultimately though, she trusted God and submitted her intellect and will to His plan, in accordance with the proverb: "Trust in the Lord with all your heart, and do not rely on your own insight" (Prov 3:5). This total submission to God, which is the perfect model of Christian discipleship, is evident in her response to the angel Gabriel, "Behold, I am the handmaid of the Lord; let it be to me according to your word" Lk 1:38.

The Humility of a Handmaid

> And [the angel Gabriel] came to her and said, "Hail, full of grace, the Lord is with you!" But she was greatly troubled at the saying, and considered in her mind what sort of greeting this might be (Lk 1:28-29).

Writing on the fitting nature of the Annunciation, Saint Thomas Aquinas wrote:

> To a humble mind nothing is more astonishing than to hear its own excellence. Now, wonder is most effective in drawing the mind's attention. Therefore the angel, desirous of drawing the Virgin's attention to the hearing of so great a mystery, began by praising her (*Summa Theologica*, III q.30 a.4 ad 1).

For human beings, a disposition of humility is one of realism—with minds prone to error and fickle hearts we are susceptible to self-deception (Jer 17:9). For philosophers, theologians, and scientists alike, a lack of humility can result in overconfidence in one's conclusions and theories. This overconfidence in turn leads to close-mindedness and stubbornness, which closes one off from correction and criticism, and a vicious cycle of perceived progress can ensue. Humility offers a satisfying alternative to this cycle, with a healthy recognition of one's limits, and makes us open to the advice of others and to modifying our thinking: "The way of a fool is right in his own eyes, but a wise man listens to advice" (Prov 12:15).

It is important to recognize that foolishness (not simply ignorance, but foolishness) can be a cause of damnation just as outright wickedness is. This is made clear in Jesus' parable about the wise and foolish virgins (Mt. 25:1-13). There is, however a direct connection between sinfulness and foolishness, and that is pride. Saint Paul pointed out this connection in his observation of the Gentiles:

> [F]or although they knew God they did not honor him as God or give thanks to him, but they became futile in their thinking and their senseless minds were darkened. Claiming to be wise, they became fools (Rm 1:21-22).

Humility enables us to get outside of ourselves and see reality as it truly is: with God at the center. As Christians, our goal should never be to glorify ourselves, but rather to help others see and experience Christ, as Saint John the Baptist did: "He must increase, but I must decrease" (Jn 3:30). Mary accomplishes this more perfectly than any other human being: "My soul magnifies the Lord" (Lk 1:46). In an similar way, the objective of philosophers and theologians should not be to achieve worldly success and the esteem of human beings, nor to be preoccupied with originality, but to discover the truth and "magnify" it by making it more accessible to others in whatever way they can. Also, when the situation demands, they should "...destroy arguments and every proud obstacle to the knowledge of God, and take every thought captive to obey Christ" (2 Cor 10:5).

The Most Effective Tool, the Most Profitable Work

Without a deep sense of wonder—wonder about ourselves, others, creation, and above all, about God—our philosophical inquiry is inevitably reduced to a mere means to finite ends, all of which are empty and unworthy of creatures made in *imago Dei*. Without humility, a false sense of certitude betrays the objectivity and openness that should belong to every lover of wisdom. Once our pursuit becomes disordered in this way, higher ideals and objects of thought are forfeited in exchange for whatever is deemed most immediately practical, pleasurable, and profitable. Philosophy is indeed a means to an end, but that end is to know the truth and to conform one's life to the truth (which is wisdom), not simply to rationalize the satisfaction of one's every desire. The honest pursuit of truth gives the human mind a strong hunger for foundational truths: universals, transcendentals, and absolutes. Truth, goodness, and beauty are the three things that we desire to possess without limit. As the eternal source of all being, God is Truth, Goodness, and Beauty itself, and is therefore above all other things worthy of our time, attention, study, and efforts to know and love. Philosophy is the greatest human tool for attaining wisdom. Theology, as the science of God, is the greatest wisdom, the "one thing needful" (Lk 10:42), and what Our Lady kept and pondered in her heart (Lk 2:19). Therefore, philosophy is not undermined, but complimented, elevated, and fulfilled whenever it serves as the handmaid of theology. She becomes a handmaid like unto the Blessed Virgin Mary. God has given all of us a mind to know the good, a heart to love the good, and a will to do the good. Let us, therefore, model our lives after Mary, the Seat of Wisdom, whose entire existence is like a song of praise to the *Summum Bonum*, the highest good conceivable, God Himself.

O you who find yourself tossed about by the storms of life, turn not your eyes from the brightness of this Star, if you would not be overwhelmed by its boisterous waves. — Bernard of Clairvaux

† Under the Mercy,

Chris Trummer

Sources:

Bernard of Clairvaux. *Sermons of St. Bernard on Advent & Christmas: Including the Famous Treatise on the Incarnation Called "Missus Est."* London; Manchester; Glasgow; New York; Cincinnati; Chicago: R. & T. Washbourne; Benziger Bros., 1909.

Catholic Biblical Association (Great Britain). *The Holy Bible: Revised Standard Version, Catholic Edition.* New York: National Council of Churches of Christ in the USA, 1994.

"Richard Dawkins - 'Why?' Questions." YouTube. April 9, 2008. Posted by: "ft790." Accessed September 5, 2015.

Thomas Aquinas. *Summa Theologica.* London: Burns Oates & Washbourne, n.d.